4

8/5

WRITING
TRUE-LIFE
STORIES

WRITING
TRUE-LIFE
STORIES

Susan C. Feldhake

PARAGON HOUSE
New York

First edition, 1993

Published in the United States by

Paragon House
90 Fifth Avenue
New York, NY 10011

Library of Congress Cataloging-in-Publication Data

Feldhake, Susan C.
    Writing true-life stories / Susan C. Feldhake.
        p.   cm.
    ISBN 1-55778-551-1
    1. Confession stories—Authorship.   I. Title.
    PN3377.5.C6F45   1992
    808'.02—dc20   92-22103
                                                    CIP

Manufactured in the United States of America

Contents

Acknowledgments

With thanks to literary agents Natasha Kern and Jerry Gross for suggesting this project and making the deal happen.

To PJ Dempsey, for guiding the effort.

To Barbara Bretton, Sylvia Kauffman, Cassie Edwards, and Jackie Smith Arnold, contacts from the past, cherished friends forever.

With grateful appreciation to the office staff of Writer's Digest School, and to the wonderful, creative, dedicated students who've taught me so much.

In appreciation for my friends and family, and Wednesday and Friday women's groups, especially those who've interacted in my life, providing grains of insight that have proven to be "grist for the mill" to keep The Muse occupied at the keyboard.

Introduction

If you want not only to become published, but to be paid—and paid well—for your work, the easiest place to find success in today's magazine market is by writing true-life stories or nonfiction personal experience articles.

There are numerous magazines that publish personal experience pieces. Their areas of interest run the gamut: Astrology, Metaphysics, New Age, Child Care, Parental Guidance, Detective, True Crime, Men's, Nature, Regional Magazines, Relationships, Alternative Life-style, Religious, True Confessions, Wildlife, Women's, etcetera.

Most of what is published in today's periodical industry is based, to some degree, in the realm of true-life, human experience. The stories and articles rolling off the presses month in and month out range from pure fiction to the unadorned truth, and all gradations in between.

While there are major differences in the slant, tone, content, philosophy, and handling of the "true"-life stories that are marketable to these diverse publications, there are also striking similarities, so work methods learned in one area will translate to another field.

An idea that would be ideal for one particular magazine with a different focus and treatment might also create a manuscript that's salable to a totally unrelated market. Therefore, after you learn the techniques, become adept at detecting a magazine's particular slant, and acquaint yourself with the targeted audience's demographic profile, you greatly increase your chances for finding success in the magazine markets.

At many publications some "literary license" is taken with just exactly how true-to-fact individual manuscripts are expected to remain when they are prepared for reader consumption. This leeway may be allowed so that they better serve the audience's interests. Sometimes stories and articles are "refocused" for readability, or clarity of comprehension, or to better illuminate the thematic content, or to neatly cameo the take-away message.

These careful alterations are not intended to erode the truthfulness of the piece but are intended to intensify the reading experience that's meant to entertain, educate, inspire, and enlighten the magazine's audience.

To accomplish all that one must in order to tailor-make irresistible "true"-life stories, it becomes necessary for authors to understand various magazines' needs. By understanding editorial requirements a writer can discern when to use straight fiction, when to use the unvarnished facts in a journalistic, newspaper-account fashion, and recognize when it's appropriate to blend the two, creating what some persons in the publishing industry call "faction," wherein factual material is presented with fiction-writing techniques so the piece reads with the pacing, and scene-by-scene, you-are-there momentum of a story or novelization, although it's really a work of nonfiction.

"True" confession magazines, in which the stories are actually fictional creations, have continued to provide the most voracious and stable market for "true-life" stories. These magazines have been around and buying stories from writers since 1919 when *True Confessions* made its debut.

Over the years probably no one market has bought more short stories than the "true" confession magazines, which peaked with upwards of forty different magazine titles printed monthly or bimonthly in the 1970s, but have now dwindled to approximately a dozen magazines, equally divided between titles aimed toward primarily black or white reading audiences.

There is still a comparatively large and steady demand for fictional personal experience stories in these magazines. Do keep in mind that these stories are *not* true. However, because they are based on real life, and their premises center on contemporary problems and conflicts, they have a ring of truth and seem as if they could quite easily have happened to someone, somewhere (and probably have).

If you want to publish for pay and also want to attain some public credit for your literary properties (confessions are written anonymously), and maybe even have a little prestige, there are hundreds of magazines from all sectors of the commercial magazine industry that use personal experience or true-life stories.

These true-life experience pieces will all contain manuscript-shaping elements of either *how it might have been, how it should have been,* or *how it could have been,* in addition to relating an event *exactly as it occurred.*

Secular Women's Magazines

Most of the major secular women's magazines like *Complete Woman, Essence, Country Woman, Ms. Magazine, Good Housekeeping,* and *Woman's World,* to name a few, now publish nonfiction, true-life, first-person viewpoint accounts whether they do it as a regular column open to free-lancers, or as individual unsolicited submissions that came in "over the transom" and fit the magazine's publishing schedule and conform to their philosophy.

Inspirational Magazines

Religious publications—*Guideposts Magazine, Aglow, Christian Herald, Christian Single, Unity Magazine, Decision, Spirit, Living With Teenagers*—are among those that use true-life, personal experience accounts. They publish a wealth of articles to inspire readers and present them with effective ways to solve their problems via applications of faith, biblical principles, or doctrinal precepts so that they might attain happier, more fulfilling and socially or spiritually harmonious lives.

Detective and True Crime

The detective and true crime magazines, like *Inside Detective, Police Yearbook, Detective Cases,* and *P.I. Magazine* are very interested in local murders, or interesting police procedural articles from your area that will be of interest to their audience nationwide.

Regional Magazines

Other markets with constant needs for personal experience pieces are the regional publications like *Chicago, Hawaii, Mississippi, The*

Native Nevadan, *"D" Magazine*, *The West Texas Star*, and others, where the situation has sharply focused geographical overtones and addresses a facet of human existence that may be peculiar to a particular area. These pieces generally run the gamut in selection of topic and treatment.

Wildlife and Sporting Magazines

Wildlife and sporting magazines like *Water, Woods, and Wildlife, Illinois Wildlife, MidWest Outdoors, Hooked on Fishing Magazine, Pacific Diver, American Skating World, Prorodeo Sports News*, etcetera, generally eschew the mundane "Joe and me"-type personal experience stories. They are, nonetheless, almost always interested in riveting true-life accounts of a fishing trip, hunting excursion, or indoor or outdoor sports event that will interest their specialized subscriberships with the piece providing some form of take-away value that will remain with readers long after they've finished perusing the article.

New Age and Unusual Phenomenon Magazines

While parapsychology and New Age philosophies promoted in such publications as *Fate, Rainbow City Express, New Realities Magazine, New Age Journal, and UFO Universe*, are not to everyone's interest, just as doctrinal applications in various denominational publications won't appeal to all readers, there is a healthy market for true-life accounts of the nature used in these magazines.

If you, or someone you know, has psychic abilities, precognitive tendencies, has dealt with unusual phenomena, seen a UFO, had a life-after-clinical-death encounter, or similar experience, these magazines provide a ready format for sharing it.

Such publications, however, want the unembellished truth exactly as the person experiencing the event perceived it. And because these kinds of periodicals are sensitive to those who would perpetrate hoaxes, they often will require that authors whose work is accepted submit a notarized statement attesting to the veracity of the manuscript.

Men's Magazines

Some men's magazines, like *Cavalier, Fling, Options, Screw, Turn-on Letters*, etcetera, seek full length "confessions" that may be either true or fictional accounts of amorous encounters. Several also pay for material to publish in the "letters" column, where writers chronicle supposedly true-life erotic escapades for the titillation of the magazine's readership. The pay tends to be very low and one magazine ceased acquiring paid free-lance material because they began to receive so many true, real-life experiences *gratis* from their regular readers!

In addition to the diverse first-person accounts, and the fictional confession markets, there is a demand for humorous treatments of real-life circumstances.

Humor Magazines

Some of the easiest stories to place are those that are slanted à la Erma Bombeck, and address topics that are based in reality that most readers can readily relate to, be it junk mail, safety caps, or the rigors of performing as the Family Tooth Fairy. Ideas arising from daily living are almost endless and they are very marketable to regional publications, opinion pages in large newspapers, and to trade journals as familiar situations are made funny and become salable because they appeal to a wide audience.

Country Woman regularly uses humor, as do many general women's magazines. Even magazines not known for using humor articles— like the beef cattlemen's publication, *Angus Journal*—will make exceptions and publish true-life humor if the topic is dead center to their readership and is guaranteed to give their audience a good laugh.

A vast number of magazines use personal experience stories that are actually factual nonfiction "true-life confessions" although they read almost identical to the fictional treatments.

Many writers, especially those new to the publishing world, often believe that nothing interesting or worth writing about has happened to them or to anyone they know. Generally, exactly the opposite is true.

There's an old saying, "You learn something new every day," and this applies to human existence. Life is a constant struggle to resolve problems and find serenity in a sometimes chaotic world that is rife with conflicts, where relationships are constantly changing, where medical advances may present ideas that were previously beyond even the realm of imagination. Day to day, God—and mankind—regularly works miracles.

Salable ideas abound if you know where to look for them in your life, in the lives of those around you, in newspapers, radio talk/call-in programs, television specials, and myriad other sources that combine to create a mother lode of possibilities for you to mine so that over the long haul you can strike it rich writing true-life stories.

After almost two decades in the publishing industry, I have sold over three hundred short stories, most of them in the "true" confession field, and I have placed in excess of one hundred articles, almost all of them somehow categorized as personal experience pieces. I have a 100 percent sales record in the confession field; I have never written a story that did not eventually sell. And in the nonfiction realm I have a track record of selling 95 percent of what I produce.

Therefore, I'm aware that my writing techniques, marketing methods, and psychological tricks to promote an atmosphere conducive to steady production, work. I feel confident recommending my methods to others who would adopt these work habits in order that they might more readily create stories and craft articles that editors will find acceptable.

The skills and techniques that I learned while writing confession stories also apply to the construction of other forms of personal experience writing. Therefore, I will cover the confession field in some depth, and then have special segments devoted to the various other forms of true-life writing.

Are you an individual who believes nothing worth writing about has ever happened to you? Even though we've probably never met, I beg to disagree with you, for I believe that you—regardless of your background, age, race, gender, religion, culture, vocation, or personal walk in life—have weathered numerous experiences that comprise the foundation for many publishable true-life accounts—either factual or fictional—that publishers will be eager to consider for publication.

By book's end, I hope to prove this to your satisfaction. And it is my hope that you will work hard, plan carefully, focus sharply, write competently, and find success as you share with others what wisdom you've acquired while coping with life's complexities.

So get prepared to examine your life—and the lives of those in the universe around you—in order that you might come up with ideas to write the true-life manuscripts that only you can create. There is an excellent chance that if you work hard, write well, slant for the specific publication, and market zealously, success can be yours.

And that's the truth . . . as I have personally experienced it.

Susan C. Feldhake
Watson, Illinois

Section I

WRITING
THE
FICTIONAL
PERSONAL
EXPERIENCE
"CONFESSION"
STORY

CHAPTER
1

The "True" Confession Field

A glance at the magazine racks in bookstores, supermarkets, marts, and convenience stores reveals that there remain about one dozen confession magazines, appearing either monthly or bimonthly, with most of them having been published regularly for decades.

These magazines, once more commonly referred to as "the pulps" because of the type of paper they're printed on, have devoted more space to short stories than any other category. With more and more "slick" magazines opting for reportorial articles the confession magazines may be the short story's last bastion.

Just as society has changed in the past decade, so have the confession publications evolved to reflect those changes.

While the blurbs on the front cover are still frequently suggestive—at times even lurid—and often promise something quite different from what's actually delivered, gone are the soft-porn confession publications of the 1970s which graphically, but euphemistically, chronicled very explicit erotic encounters, often at the expense of any recognizable story line.

At the time, these magazines' titillation factor was guaranteed to sell copies. But with the arrival of R- and X-rated movies, videos, and even spicy daytime television dramas that offered easily accessible racy action, persons no longer had to turn to the "hide-under-the-mattress" confession magazines for risqué reading material as they did in generations gone by.

The remaining hard-core confession readership, which is vast enough to dictate press runs ranging from 100,000 to 250,000 copies per issue, is more concerned with basic values and they prefer interesting, plot-driven, emotion-laden, memorable stories and characters that they can identify with.

Therefore, content ranges from squeaky clean and wholesome tales to an occasional racy story where most of the romantic action is off-stage and is left to readers' imaginations.

1.1 Know Your Reader—The Editor Does

Editors are aware that readers have high expectations and they want stories that are strongly constructed, have good motivation, realistic dialogue and characterization, a solid conflict, plausible resolution, and insights that offer a valid take-away message to the readership.

Generally all confession magazines slant their products toward a working-class audience comprised of women ages 18–35. The bulk of the readership for confession magazines consists of women who are high school or college students, homemakers, divorcées, or older women.

Editors look for stories where women are shown as being professional, independent, intelligent, assertive, and don't need a man to give them an identity but who can still enjoy being romanced.

Confession publishers are very sensitive to reader input that usually arrives in letters to the editor. If they spot a trend in the mail they receive, they capitalize on the suggestions or seek to address complaints, and this can bring prompt changes in guidelines.

1.2 Preparing to Write 'Em Right

Authors who are serious about writing for the confessions should send self-addressed stamped envelopes to the editors' attention and request current guidelines. Writers should also purchase copies of the magazines—or if they're unavailable locally send a check or money order to buy sample copies direct from the publishers—and read the stories and study the advertisements so that they can discern the subtle differences in philosophy and focus among the various confession magazines.

There are certain mechanical aspects to consider. All confession stories are written in the first-person point-of-view, the "I" view-point. The narrator can be either male or female, but stories told from the woman's point-of-view are far more likely to sell than those narrated by a male character, although stories purportedly by men do sell well.

In the confession field simultaneous submissions are not acceptable because these magazines purchase all rights. Story releases or contracts wherein the author sells away the rights for an agreed-upon fee are signed before the piece will be printed, but editors don't wish to take the time to consider a story and offer to buy it, only to learn that a competitor has already spoken for the manuscript. It usually takes several months for an editor to decide yes or no about a manuscript, and after a piece is accepted for publication, it may be several additional months before it appears in print. This period could extend beyond that if it's a seasonal manuscript. Holiday-related stories should be submitted six months before that issue to give the editors a time frame within which to work.

1.3 Recognizing Magazines' Similarities and Diversities

All confession magazines use from eight to twelve stories in each issue. The general women's magazines, if they print fiction at all (and many do not) publish only a token short story per issue. For free-lancers that means if you happen to sell a short story to a major women's magazine—while the pay rate is impressive—it's going to be the only check you'll see from them for a long, long time, unless you're an author of such stature that your name is already a household word. Such big league magazines don't want to reuse the same author—especially an unknown—too often.

Both Lexington Library, Inc., and Macfadden Women's Group rely on outside writers, as they're 100 percent free-lance, whereas in the past editors frequently assigned stories to treasured writers so they could do away with the overhead of mining the "slush pile" (unsolicited manuscripts) for suitable stories to print. At a few houses, editors were expected to "staff write" stories for publication.

Fictional confessions are anonymously published with no genuine byline giving you, the author, public credit for having written a particular story.

Macfadden Women's Group, publishers of the various magazines known in the industry as "The Trues," dispense with any form of story credit, but Lexington Library, Inc., publishing for the black audience, uses "bylines." They are every bit as fictional as the stories, however, as Lexington Library authors are instructed to isolate the "I" narrator's given name in the story (type it beneath the title) so that the editor won't have to search through the manuscript hunting for a reference to the character's name to edit in a tag line beneath the title.

The confession magazines, because they are not concerned with the author's true identity—except for the company's comptroller to get it correctly on the checks—appreciate authors that they can count on to sell them stories month after month, year-in, year-out.

1.4   Confession Writing: What's in It for You?

Editors are always on the lookout for talented writers because although there may be a solid core unit of writers, there is always attrition, and they have a need to cultivate ongoing crops of writers to replace those who've left the field for one reason or another. Some especially good authors may find that they are able to sell more than one story a month to an editor. I once picked up a copy of a confession magazine and discovered that six of the stories in that issue were mine!

If you multiply the number of current confession magazines times an average ten stories per issue per month, you will quickly see why the confession field creates a constant need for the romantic "true" experience short story.

Most writers, when they decide to try their hand at writing, have not only an urge to write stories but also possess a strong desire to earn money. It's not surprising, therefore, that in studying the markets and learning that the confession field comprises what's long been recognized as the easiest, best paying place to break in, almost all authors at one time or another try writing the "true" confession story.

Many writers begin crafting confessions solely as a steady source of income. Others see the field as a great place to gain writing credits to use elsewhere, others as a way to get some editorial input, while still others view it as an "earn while you learn" opportunity. Plus, there are authors who write confessions as a way to relax after a day spent working on novels. For them the money is convenient, but the psychological aspects of quick acceptances and regular success can be very valuable to a novelist who is laboring over a book that may not reap rewards for months—even years—to come.

For many years the annual cost of living has increased. Unfortunately in the confession field, payment has decreased, but the field still remains one of the better paying areas for authors who want to write and sell short stories.

Lexington Library, Inc., pays a flat fee of $75–100 per story ranging from 17–19 double-spaced pages, with each story having an obligatory two love scenes. Both are very brief (several paragraphs) and do not show the sex act but allude to it. The Trues pay from 3–5 cents per word, and want stories from 1500 to 6000 words, up to 8000 for novelettes, which can result in a substantial check. Both confession publishers remit payment usually on, or shortly after, publication.

You don't need any special qualifications or background to write confessions.

1.5 Professional Confession Writers: Who Are We?

Veteran "true story" writers come from all segments of society, range in education from high school dropouts to college-educated professionals, hail from bucolic rural America, or metropolitan areas with skyscrapers blocking the horizon from sight. Because they vary so greatly in their individual life-styles, how they view problems and arrive at solutions, for instance, their ideas can be extremely interesting and different, even if they happen to be developing the same basic idea. They all generally have in common a love of people and feel a bit of responsibility toward mankind's lot. They have a desire to make life easier and may have a knack for coming up with workable solutions to problems.

Although these can't be called requisites necessary for confession writing, personality traits that successful confession writers tend to share, which seem to help them excel, regardless of how different their personal backgrounds, are a sensitivity to emotional reactions, curiosity about the world and people around them, a talent for analytical thinking, a capacity to face and solve problems, a genuine interest in others, the ability to understand even those people who are not always easy to like, and a knack for storytelling that allows them to make an everyday situation riveting enough to hold reader attention from start to finish.

1.6 Basic Requirements to Launch Your Confession Writing Career

If you want to create a niche for yourself in the confession field you don't need anything special to start writing true-life stories except for the desire to do so. And of course you'll need to arm yourself with the rudimentary tools all writers require in order to professionally approach the marketplace.

To get started you need: paper, carbon, mailing envelopes, and an elite or pica typewriter, with an acceptable typeface. ("Script" machines are not acceptable.) It's even better if you have access to a "dedicated" word processor, or a computer with word processing capabilities, and a good printer, either daisywheel, laser, or at the very least, near-letter-quality dot matrix. These tools will allow you to prepare a suitable submission package because hand-written, single-spaced stories will be returned unread. And you'll need stamps—lots of stamps—for all publishers require a SASE (often referred to as a "sassy," the acronym for Self-Addressed, Stamped Envelope), for the editor will use it to return your story to you if your offering doesn't happen to fit her magazine's needs.

So take heart! If you educate yourself about the mechanics of confession writing, follow the professional rules for marketing, have a bit of storytelling talent to develop, will foster the right attitudes and are willing to work hard, there's every reason to believe that success in the confession field can be yours.

CHAPTER
2

How to Find Appropriate Ideas

When it comes to the confession field, ideas are bountiful, but authors must train themselves to "think confession" so that they'll be able to regularly recognize and pluck the salable situations from the clusters of timely ideas that they will encounter on a daily basis.

Then authors must preserve the harvest in a notebook, creating a storehouse of short story material to consume when the future seems to produce a barren season, as sometimes happens even to the most prolific authors who are toiling in the vineyards of true experience writing.

2.1 Why a Good Idea Isn't Enough

Coming up with a good idea, unfortunately, isn't enough, for the treatment of a topic is the all-important factor that determines whether an editor accepts or rejects a manuscript. The exact same idea, depending on how it is processed by the author, can result in a tale that is trite, hackneyed, and deemed unacceptable, or it can be handled so that its treatment is fresh, unique and results in a quick sale.

While there are exceptions, it's rare for a beginning confession writer to connect with the first story or two written and submitted in the confession field because they are often flawed. Fortunately most writers, once they learn the ropes, are able to go back, revise these learning efforts, and make them salable.

Usually these initial attempts meet with rejection because editors deem that they are "contrived," "lacking in sufficient motivation," "don't seem realistic," are "too predictable," are considered "old hat," or "the idea has been written into the ground" by previous writers who, instinctively, seemed to select that exact story line and resolution for their debut.

Quirky as it seems, frequently authors' first confession story ideas will be the premise of a husband, who is suspected by his wife of having a love affair, but is really using the "other woman"—who appears very guilty—to help him concoct a wonderful surprise (like a mink coat, trip to Hawaii, or exquisite piece of jewelry) for his suspicious wife who has conveniently "forgotten" all about her birthday or their upcoming wedding anniversary. This story is guaranteed to receive a rejection slip no matter how well written it is because of its predictability.

2.2   Why You Must Develop the Basic Idea

It's important for those who would plot confession stories to take pains to process the idea so that the unexpected—not the anticipated—is what actually happens.

We read stories not to find out what we know is going to happen but to discover that what we'd expected to take place isn't what transpires. Being "fooled" keeps us interested, it builds suspense, and creates a satisfying, fulfilling, and entertaining reading experience.

Therefore, in settling upon ideas, consider your options, and be prepared to reject the very first plot or two that your imagination offers because very probably that's the chain of events and final outcome others have hit upon, too.

You must stretch your imagination, mull over unusual possibilities, and then craft the story so that the logical sequence of events not only seems possible but likely to happen as you've conceived it.

2.3   Mining the Mother Lode of Your Experience

Although the desire to write confessions may be strong, for many new authors there may be an acute sense of frustration at the outset. They can be all primed to write fictional personal experience stories, are eager to get started, but suddenly they can't come up with what feels like even one idea about which to write.

Perhaps you, too, would argue that you've lived a rather tame life.

Nothing exciting, shocking, or provocative has ever happened to you. You might be absolutely right. But it certainly won't prevent you from writing salable confession stories.

There are an almost unlimited number of subjects for you to explore and make conform to the confession field's needs, and you can do it with finesse and no embarrassing qualms, if you keep in mind that the "real you" is not confessing. You're simply the conduit for the countless fictional narrators in your imagination to tell their true-life stories. Perhaps their basic situations arise from total fabrications on your part, or maybe they're actually grounded in reality, or somewhere in between. The choice is up to you.

2.4 Profit from Others' Experiences

Your life is uneventful? Then take a look around you. The town's "bad girl" has a story to tell. Or what about your classmates from high school? Then there are those interesting individuals whose paths crossed with yours while in college, in the workplace, in a fraternal organization, or even that stranger in the checkout lane at the supermarket whose conversation with a companion was so intriguing to overhear.

Borrow their problems, their solutions, their weaknesses, their strengths, the triumphs they've found in life, the tragedies they've faced. Change the basic details, rearrange them, shield identities to protect their privacy, then live out their problem in your imagination, analyzing how you might have a character make a wiser choice than the real-life individual did, and go from there. Focus on a basic premise, then "live it out" in your imagination, mentally trying out several possible chains of events. Select the one that's most unusual—but also the most logical—then write it.

Even with a coterie of interesting friends and acquaintances who are having, or have had, unusual and exciting experiences that may spark story ideas, confession writers who want to remain in the field must constantly come up with timely, innovative topics for their stories. This means that most of us have to look beyond the experiences of friends and family.

Medical columns, carried by most daily newspapers, are an excellent source of material. Such startling things as sex change operations, hormonal diseases, pseudocyesis (false pregnancy), allergy to semen, frigidity, impotence, infertility, test-tube babies, surrogate motherhood, sex surrogates, artificial insemination, even auto-erotic asphyxiation have been mentioned in medical columns and were used by me to create manuscripts that sold in the confession field.

In addition to creating riveting stories centering on provocative topics, because I researched the symptoms, treatments, and in some case legal and moral ramifications, and worked these details into the story, the magazines' readers were educated as they were entertained. Research can be a key word.

2.5   Researching the Medical-Based Confession Story

Frequently, information gleaned from a bona fide medical column, or gained by listening to a victim of a medical malady hold forth about his or her symptoms while explaining the standard treatment, will give you sufficient knowledge to plot a workable resolution and offer solid take-away information to the readership.

Many times a medical-based story can be related so that its treatment doesn't render it necessary to include intricate explanations. However, if a story hinges on a specific medical aspect it is vitally important to ensure accuracy, so use words from the technical lexicon, explain their meanings, and be certain that any words used are spelled right and are used correctly. Such precise attention to detail does much to reassure the editor of your credibility. If you spell a word wrong, or use a term incorrectly, the editor will wonder what other technical errors you might be making that she's not noticed because it's beyond her personal realm of knowledge.

If you don't know something for a fact in a medical-based story, then it's up to you to consult with those individuals who do, and this can be accomplished with a quick call to your family doctor, or with a note accompanied by a Self-Addressed, Stamped Envelope. If you don't want to trouble your physician, ask a friend who is a nurse; she or he probably would be delighted to help you, especially if you reciprocate with a thoughtful gift certificate, or dinner out.

In my experience, persons I've contacted for technical advice have been honored that I've singled them out for questions in their field of expertise, and they were enthusiastic about being able to help. But if you feel shy about contacting professionals in their field (as many unpublished authors are), with a little legwork you can often find the information on your own by making the best use of the nationwide library system, especially if you know your way around the card catalog and stacks.

2.6   Using a Professional Researcher

If you're not comfortable researching and the idea is so timely you don't want someone to beat you to it, you might wish to enlist the services of a professional researcher. Because it's a researcher's daily business to locate answers, they're adept at doing so and often have vast, in-home libraries. They are true professionals at availing themselves of all that libraries offer and a good researcher can locate in a matter of minutes what could take an average person days. Most charge an hourly fee, prorated to the actual time involved, and their services—if they help you sell a story—could be a bargain, and the cost of this overhead is tax-deductible. If it's a timely topic, and you have to dig a bit for information—or hire it done—it almost guarantees that the editor has not seen the idea before and therefore will respond with a prompt and positive reaction.

Trade journals for nurses and doctors are available and you needn't be a member of the medical community to subscribe to them. Many technical articles will be beyond a layman's understanding, but "letters to the editor" columns in medical publications, and those where subscribers write in to share their unusual health care-related experiences, could spark stories to the extent that a yearly subscription fee is a small price to pay for the chance to garner such a wealth of ideas. Not everyone can, or wants, to write medical stories, although they have proven to be very popular over the decades. In that case, be sure to get out in public.

2.7   Eavesdropping for Fun and Money

Surround yourself with people and so many ideas may drop at your feet that all you have to do is take the time to pick them up.

Some years ago I was at a cocktail party where a young woman, a complete stranger to me then and now who'd been married for several years, was confiding to another guest how deeply she'd been hurt when her mother-in-law, who very much wanted a grandchild, accused the young woman of sneaking birth control pills to keep from getting pregnant.

I was moved by her poignant story, and touched by her deep hurt at being unfairly accused about something that I felt wasn't her mother-in-law's business to question.

That evening an idea was planted—and took root—but it was some weeks before the story blossomed. And when it did, it was in quite a different form from the true-life experience that had been inspired by an individual's personal confession. I doubt she'd have even "recognized herself" in the final product.

In my story, "Haunted by My Mother's Past," I had a young woman who elopes with a soldier she'd met not long before, a man who loved children and wants several. When the happy couple returns home with the deed done, her mother takes her aside and tells her the truth: her real father is not the man she'd called "Dad" all those years—her biological father is actually the mildly retarded street sweeper, an aging man by then, who'd raped her mother when she was a teenager.

Because the young bride fears that she has bad genes, and is terrified by the idea that she'll bear a mentally disabled child, she sneaks birth control pills. She doesn't trust her new husband enough to tell him the truth so they can reach a joint decision and come to terms with the problem. The narrator only finds the courage to tell her husband the truth after he discovers her birth control pills and he's hurt, betrayed, angry, and she realizes that her only shot at happiness is to set about righting her wrongs. She admits the sordid truth—explaining her motivations—so that he can understand why she behaved as she did and even empathize. At the resolution the couple consults with a doctor who is able to assure them that her genetic makeup is not a problem, and that they have an excellent chance of bearing healthy, perfectly normal children.

2.8   Local Sources for Timely Ideas

Therefore, an evening spent flipping through old high school yearbooks, sipping coffee and eavesdropping in a restaurant, taking part in chitchat at cocktail parties, attending church suppers or family gatherings, can provide myriad provocative and emotion-packed ideas to serve as the foundation for memorable confession stories.

These ideas, *when changed*, make wonderful problems for confession stories because they arise out of true-life, personal experiences in the realm of average human existence. When you use real life as the basis for a story, it is imperative that you change the details. Use a different locale and line of work. Fabricate new identities and a totally unrelated family system. Be sure to thoroughly camouflage real-life places and people to protect their privacy . . . and your legal good health . . . so that individuals who spark ideas within you would never recognize themselves.

2.9   Spotting Ideas in the Print Media

Newspapers and magazines that carry "personal" ads in the classified section—*Grit*, *New York Magazine*, *Saturday Review*, *Mother Earth News*, and various singles' publications—are another wonderful source for ideas. Just when you believe you've seen it all, you'll discover a nugget that you've never encountered, not even in your wildest flights of fancy, and it cries out to become your next short story.

The question-and-answer columns, advice columns, and letters to the editor in such magazines as *Good Housekeeping*, *McCall's*, *Cosmopolitan*, *SELF Magazine*, *Ladies' Home Journal*, *Woman's World*, and *Ms. Magazine*, to name a few, are all super places to look for story gems.

I've found some of my best ideas in *Time* magazine, which has regular weekly columns devoted to specific areas of interest to our general society. Not long ago, an issue of *Time* carried a full-page piece chronicling how popular video cameras were becoming and how they encouraged people to make unusual home videos for their viewing enjoyment and touted the joys of being able to relive precious moments—the experience not unlike being able to flip through a photo album.

The reporter covering the piece for *Time* had interviewed couples who'd either bought video cameras, or rented the equipment, and they and their spouses set up the hardware in their bedrooms and with the camera whirring filmed themselves making love. In the body of this report, a recently widowed woman gave a quote that explained the comfort derived from the video memento of she and her husband making love.

I read the piece with great interest—but more than a bit of

apprehension, too—shuddering when I considered the ramifications if the steamy, home-grown "blue movie" videotape cassette got into the wrong hands.

I plotted and wrote the story within twenty-four hours, photocopied the page from *Time*, enclosed it with my submission, and before my next issue of *Time* could arrive in my mailbox I received a letter of acceptance from the editor who knew a timely story when she saw one.

Generally a writer will have less competition using a short news item, or a local one, than a piece which has been given wide national coverage. If you choose to use one given coast-to-coast attention, it's a good idea to execute the idea *immediately*. When gathering ideas for the future, as you mine your local daily newspaper for ideas, look for the regional news items that probably won't be given space in newspapers in other geographical areas so you're not thrown into what could become a race against time with other professional confession writers.

The advice columns, be they those with nationwide exposure, or restricted to your own area, where people can bear their souls, present their most intimate problems, air pet peeves, ask for help, or warn others about bad situations, are all excellent sources for story material.

But rarely will one letter give an author a full-blown premise for a plot. When combined, however, an element from one letter added to an event from another, linked with a motivation from another, tied in with advice from yet another letter, can construct a viable story.

2.10   Tailoring the Topic's Treatment to Fit the Market

If you want to write for the confession magazines that focus on a younger, late-teen audience, then you should acquaint yourself with what's of interest to modern teenagers and what problems they face in contemporary society. Teen magazines carry great articles and their advice columns and letters to the editor section are gold mines of opportunity.

Keep in mind if you're writing for teenagers that editors feel an obligation to guide our nation's youth, and hope through examples in the stories they publish to educate teens who'll recognize the voice of experience within stories so that they can learn from others' mistakes, or be inspired to emulate the story characters' triumphant actions and ante up such efforts themselves.

2.11   Handling Sensitive Topics in Good Taste

Every time I am faced with the details of the death of a teenage boy, found hanging, whether I hear about it on the radio, see it on television, read of it in the newspaper, or am told by a friend, my heart goes out to the grief-stricken parents—and to the teenage boy—as I realize one more youth has likely fallen prey to the idea of experiencing a heightened sexual act only to find accidental death.

I tend to be a rather frank individual, and when such an accidental hanging happened in our area, I made a point of suppressing squeamishness, and hoping that I sounded casual, I mentioned the sadness of the death to my son and his teenage friends, and explained how the boy had accidentally suffocated while trying a rope trick during an auto-erotic act that had been periodically promoted in various men's magazines over the years as a nifty sexual experience.

I wanted to make sure that my son and his friends realized that there were great risks involved in what they could be hearing from friends in the locker room—reportedly a thrilling masturbatory experience.

When within a year's time there were two more such deaths in our region, I decided to "go public" with a personal campaign, and I concluded that perhaps the platform found in the confession magazines would be an ideal place to educate youngsters that kids can *die* when going in search of the ultimate orgasm.

It was a topic that was timely, one not easily handled, and involved several days to figure out how to relate the story so that it'd be tasteful enough not to offend even the most squeamish reader, relieve the story of even a patina of tawdriness, manage to create the all-important "sympathetic narrator" required in confessions, and offer a convincing and valuable take-away message to remain with readers long after they'd finished the story.

I knew at the outset that I could hardly use as my viewpoint character the boy who was going to die with a rope around his neck as he gave himself sexual pleasure, because in the confession field the hero or heroine has obviously "lived to tell about it."

The various confession requisites, combined with logic, resulted in the story, "They're Blaming Me for My Boyfriend's Death!"

In the story a high school girl intends to remain a virgin, and her boyfriend abides by her wishes. Occurring totally "off-stage," and related in a quick passage of narrative, the surrounding details come out: The boy's parents are divorced, his father is something of a swinger, and when the youth spends some time in a distant state with his dad during his summer vacation, he discovers some sleazy men's magazines, reads directions instructing him how to perform the sex trick, and his father comes home from work to find him a victim of accidental hanging.

The girl who has lost her boyfriend is devastated, and her grief is made worse when the youth's father, after the funeral, accuses her of causing his son's death because she wasn't being intimate with him, so the boy attended to his needs and died. After talking to a counselor, and being reassured by the dead youth's mother, the girl realizes it was not her fault, that we're all responsible for our own decisions and actions, and that the dead boy's father was actually lashing out at her in his own guilty grief for his part in his son's death.

Without getting maudlin and becoming offensive in the details, the story *did* get the point across that such actions are potentially fatal.

I felt that the story had managed to convey everything I'd set out to accomplish to enlighten readers. Apparently the editor I submitted it to agreed, for two days after I'd mailed it I received an excited telephone call. She was enthusiastic as she accepted the piece, congratulated me on the message, and was elated to feature a story with such a solid take-away message. This editor was receptive also, because she, too, had become concerned about the growing problem of auto-erotic asphyxiation deaths nationwide.

While I was paid quickly, and paid well, my greatest reward in writing this particular story is being able to believe that perhaps somewhere there are youths who remain alive and well, now growing into mature manhood because they learned what men's magazines that sometimes promote the rope trick don't always tell them: people can die when going in search of dangerous thrills.

2.12 Collecting Brilliant Ideas from the Boob Tube

Network television talk shows and Public Broadcasting System in-depth specials can offer great ideas or simply provide background information to make a story believable. A video cassette recorder to preserve the footage and assist in research is a wonderful tool to allow authors to absorb ideas at their leisure.

Even cartoons can be a good place to search for solid ideas. Generally cartoon material must be universal to appeal to a cross-section of readers, and if it's got a wide enough base to work for getting a laugh, it'll generally translate to the confession field where it can tug at the heart strings.

2.13 Using the Confession Magazines as an Idea Source

Perhaps the easiest place to get confession ideas from is confession magazines themselves. While veteran confession writers don't always take time to read the stories in the magazines that they write for after they've learned the craft and started to sell with regularity, it's assured that they'll scan the covers and peruse titles and accompanying blurbs.

So go to the local newsstand with a notebook. Look through that month's offering of confession publications. Jot down story blurbs and titles that appeal to you. For some, a full-blown story to fit the title may arrive at once. Quickly scribble down the details, then move on. Plot the sketchy skeletons for your stories as fast as you can—without opening the magazines to get any clues as to plot content. Do this for as many stories as you are able. Then purchase the magazine, go home, and begin reading.

Filtered through your personal perceptions and philosophies and plotted along the circuits of your unique imagination, chances are excellent you've just come up with a lot of stories that are totally unrelated to the published pieces, and ones that when in final form will fit the needs of the confession field.

2.14   Create a Title—Then Find the Idea
to Fit It

On a day when you really don't feel like writing, another helpful exercise is to grab your notebook and make up your own list of provocative titles—as if you were an editor creating catchy blurbs for the magazine's cover. Given time, your subconscious will do the rest and one day you'll awaken with the perfect confession story to fit your title.

There is an "art" to coming up with confession titles. Some titles are tender, others are provocative, some are sad, but all of them have an undercurrent of emotion, and more than a few have sexual overtones that frequently promise more than they deliver, as they're boldly displayed on colorful confession covers to tempt the reader to purchase that issue.

A random sampling to help you get the feel for creating your own titles to nudge your subconscious to plot stories that fit:

> *WITHOUT WARNING—I never suspected my dream date would end the night raping me!*
> *FANTASY LOVER—When my husband stopped making love to me, I found the perfect substitute!*
> *DEAR DIARY: My first time wasn't as exciting as I had expected it to be.*
> *NO SHAME: I was having an affair with my son's best friend.*
> *EX-LOVER—He threatened to tell my husband everything!*
> *PHONE SEX—I liked talking dirty to boys!*
> *PRIVATE HELL—I was hopelessly addicted to sex.*
> *I SPENT MY WEDDING DAY IN JAIL.*
> *MY HUSBAND CAME BACK FROM THE DEAD.*
> *SEX ADDICT—How could I have married him?*
> *I'LL MAKE HIM FORGET HIS WIFE now that he's my lover.*
> *BROKEN LOVE PROMISES—Why do I keep coming back for more?*

So get ready to try your hand at writing provocative titles of your own and you'll discover how fun and inspiring it is.

Come up with a dynamite title—so the editor won't have to rename your story (as frequently happens unless you create such great titles that the editor knows she can't do better)—and your manuscript's title page alone will set the editor to thinking in terms of accepting your story because she'll start envisioning such a super title emblazoned on her magazine's cover to pique consumers to buy the issue and enjoy the story behind such a provocative tag.

2.15 Enjoy Staying Power by Staying Current

Once you get "in" with a confession editor, you have a direct line to learning her up-to-the-moment needs. Editors regularly revamp their guidelines to reflect a change in needs, and they're prone to give authors in their stable a quick telephone call to alert them to what they'd like to see so authors can begin thinking in those terms. They also will warn writers away from specific treatments to prevent the pros in their stable from wasting time on stories that are devoted to situations that have become passé because they're seen with such regularity that it guarantees a rejection slip no matter how wonderful the writing is. Readers want fresh, exciting, unusual stories, not a rehash of what they might have read six months ago.

Editors don't revise guidelines on a whim, they do it when they get enough information for the data to convince them that there is a trend among readers. Perhaps their most valuable indicator is the mail that stories in their magazine generate, for they are aware that there are industry equations that they can "plug-in" and know that for every letter reacting in a specific way, X-number of readers also feel that way but have not taken the time to write a letter of protest or affirmation.

Therefore it's a good idea for confession writers, even if they're too busy to read all the confession stories published every month to set aside the time required to analyze what's in the "letters to the editor" column.

Some typical reader comments:

. . . After I read this story, I almost cried. I think it was one of the best you've ever printed. I hope you will print more stories like this in the future.

After reading this story, I cried. I am just like Christina. I just hope I can learn to have self-confidence and learn to love myself once again. Thanks for printing this story.

. . . This story touched me. I just had a baby boy . . . and I don't think I could've handled what happened to her. Thank you for printing this story. It made me realize that child stealing really does happen. I'll be careful, believe me!

I really felt that Becky got off too easy. She should have gotten punished for lying to her parents. If she got away with leaving once—even if a teacher was there—she'll do it again.

Becky's parents should've been glad that she was with the band she was with. You only have to listen to the news reports and you'll know she could've been hanging around with some band members a whole lot worse!

I've been reading your magazine for thirty-one years, and I'm so glad you don't allow language and pictures that are in poor taste in your magazine.

I found myself admiring the author tremendously. Her story really moved me. People like her will always be remembered in my prayers.

I started reading your magazine when I was eleven and a half. It kind of gets you ready for your grown up years.

Billie is a spoiled woman, and I know that she and Brock will not have lasting happiness. Even though they just got married, I hope he finds a woman who'll really appreciate him someday! I had an (ex) sister-in-law like Billie. Thank God my brother is now married to a gal we all love!

While the letters published usually pertain to stories that readers especially enjoyed, and may contain bits of advice that they wish to have passed along to the heroines (who they believe are real individuals struggling with 100 percent true problems), editors do get some "brickbats" and they're very sensitive to stories that readers do not enjoy or feel offered solutions with which readers seemed unable to agree because either the characters got off too easily, or were excessively punished.

With their "finger on the readers' pulse" editors can help authors tailor future stories so they come up with resolutions that will appeal to the average rank-and-file reader. Editors will also learn what types of stories to shy away from acquiring so they don't risk their readers—many of whom mention having read the magazine consistently for an impressive number of years—switching their loyalties to a competitor's publications.

Editors not only keep in mind their readers' likes and dislikes, but they also work to establish close relationships with writers that they realize they can rely on to provide them with publishable stories. Between readers and writers there is a need for literary middle-men, and editors perform this vital service by linking the reading consumer with the writing supplier. By serving in this capacity, editors can also nurture loyalty from authors who'll submit to their magazine title instead of to a competitor's magazine.

Recently a confession editor gave me such a call providing the information for my own use, and she also asked me to pass it on to the students I was working with in my capacity as a Writer's Digest School correspondence instructor. A number of the students in my care, whose initial ideas had seemed tailor-made for the confession field, had gone on to sell works to this specific editor after we'd perfected their stories for the market.

"We're seeing too much infidelity," she said. "With AIDS and sexually transmitted diseases such a problem today, we'd like to focus more on monogamous relationships. Also, we're looking for the villainous woman story—an 'Alexis type'—who could end up getting hurt by the one she's hurt. We all enjoy seeing the characters we 'love to hate' get their just comeuppances. We're also more open to adventure, intrigue, and total woman stories that reflect today's contemporary society. We are interested in seeing stories about upwardly mobile readers—women who are career-oriented, maybe entrepreneurs—in love with men who are doctors, lawyers, or other professional people. Sports figures could be of interest, too. And while we are slanting toward the younger career woman in her mid-twenties, we want teens and older women to be able to identify also. In short, we want fresh ideas within these areas. If a story's a bit out of the ordinary—we definitely want to see it."

This editor also had concrete ideas about what they didn't want to see.

"There have been too many rape stories. Generally, we don't want to see stories where rape is a plot element, although the right handling of date rape might work, since it's a timely topic. We don't want any more student and teacher affairs. Even before the Pamela Smart trial thing we'd been inundated with these, and since then such submissions have increased. Also, we're tired of stories where a girlfriend or wife discovers that her boyfriend is gay or transsexual. Those have been done into the ground in past years. Also, no country girl arriving in the big, bad city to be turned out on the streets by a slick-talking pimp. And please spare us the 'he stole my money, he stole my heart' stories."

Rest assured that viable ideas are all around you, waiting to be recognized and developed into full blown stories. Someday, friends and family, who'll read your stories and be captivated by the topics and plot lines, are almost guaranteed to look at you with amazed expressions, and ask in awed tones, "Where on earth do you get your ideas?!"

You'll know that you've really succeeded when they don't detect the vital part they may have played in assisting your career by helping provide you with situations about which to write.

But rather than come clean when you're asked about the source of your unusual stories, in the best interests of all concerned let me give you a tip:

When someone inquires, "Where do you get your ideas?" simply smile and say, "I order them wholesale from a supplier in St. Louis. . . ."

CHAPTER
3

Shaping the Idea into a Theme

There may seem to be innumerable mistakes in life to "confess" about, but in actuality these true-life stories are all merely variations on a limited number of basic ways to "err." As a result the narrator learns valuable lessons, however, after striving to correct problems caused through poor choices.

Confession writers learn quickly that there is really "nothing new under the sun." There are only fresh ways to handle old problems that have been with us since the dawn of history. Yet there are other premises that are as new as tomorrow, and have become possible only because of scientific technology that gives a modernistic spin to the same basic human conflicts dating back to the origins of mankind.

3.1 Setting Your Story's Boundaries

What makes each story different and timely, no matter how eternal the human difficulty, is the development of its theme.

Depending on personal background, philosophy, cultural environment, religious indoctrination, or any number of mitigating factors, the same basic problem can be resolved in as many different ways as there are individuals tackling that situation.

Selecting a specific theme to develop lays down the philosophical parameters within which the story will be told. It creates a "pattern" for the story to follow as it logically unfolds, and a theme also marks an invisible boundary within which to contain the narrator's actions.

3.2   Must You Have a Theme?

There are those who say that it isn't necessary to have a theme to create a successful story, and they sometimes maintain that literary analysts would ruin the enjoyment of reading audiences by teaching them to look for meanings and symbolism that aren't really there. So perhaps it's not required that all stories have themes but it is a requisite in the confession field, where editors must have a reason for the story to be shared with their readership and where take-away value is a prime consideration.

3.3   Selecting the Best Theme for Your Story

For authors who want to succeed in the confession field, it's important to consider themes before you begin writing—not after you've concluded a manuscript—and then look back to try to detect some kind of rhyme and reason linking the events contained within the plot sequence. Such a haphazard, hit-or-miss method almost guarantees the need for massive revisions that can be avoided by utilizing sufficient pre-writing considerations.

Basically, the theme of any story is the specific point, or "moral," that an author wishes to illustrate by arranging cause-and-effect factors within the plot. In that way through the conflicts encountered, the choices the narrator makes, and the success with which the problem is resolved, cause-and-effect action will either prove—or disprove—the theory as set forth in the story's structure.

The incorporation of a theme into the story should never be obvious—like waving a flag—because to do so detracts from the natural flow of the tale and makes it seem more like pompous, self-righteous sermonizing than the entertaining escapism most readers desire when they sit down to read. Themes should always be introduced in as natural, logical, and unobtrusive a manner as possible.

A strong theme should arise from the story as a whole, like interlocking links, and not consist of a tacked on "moral" which can disrupt the flow of fiction by seeming like a didactic lecture. Ideally, a theme should be a subtle but powerful statement that's borne out through characters' action and dialogue. It need not necessarily be narrated anywhere as a "motto to live by," although in many stories the summation of the theme *is* presented in a brief "statement" in the come-to-realize scene at the story's climax, usually either through dialogue or narrative introspection.

When providing examples of themes, certain common phrases are frequently called into use. But do keep in mind that all themes do not read like adages, and do not necessarily translate with the succinctness of a fable's "moral of the story."

Once you know your theme, and you may have chosen the point you wish to make before you write—as I did in the piece dealing with auto-erotic asphyxiation where I worked with the theme that thrill-seeking could be fatal—the story may seem to plot itself.

There are other times when you may have a fascinating situation, interesting characters, and it is only after you begin writing that you discover a theme is beginning to emerge. Once you detect the presence of a theme, you can safeguard it and have it show up like a thread woven throughout a tapestry to give it strength and unity.

Frequently themes can be stated in one succinct line and may have a ring of familiarity because they often sound like adages, or "old saws" we've grown up with:

"Truth is stranger than fiction."

"Pride goeth before a fall."

"The truth will out."

"Seek and you shall find."

"There are none so blind as those who refuse to see."

"Birds of a feather flock together."

"Those who lie down with dogs arise with fleas."

"Beauty is only skin deep—nastiness goes to the bone."

"Good will triumph over evil."

"A stitch in time saves nine."

"What goes 'round comes around."

"What's sauce for the goose is sauce for the gander."

Your stories' themes probably will not be so patently pigeon-holed nor should they be. Occasionally a story can fit a familiar thematic phrase, but as many, or more, do not.

Themes are not absolutes and sometimes the best and most memorable stories are those that would work to disprove a commonly accepted bit of wisdom.

3.4 Creating Story Strength by Developing Multiple Themes

It's not unusual to write stories where there are several strong, overlapping themes. These pieces are almost always so interesting and well-structured that editors will receive them with delight.

Such was the case with my story, "Jealous Lover," published by Lexington Library, Inc.

The major theme was that "jealousy kills love." An accompanying message was that "obsession may try to masquerade as love." Another point made in the same story was "family is where, when you go there, they have to let you in." And all of this dovetailed with my personal philosophy that we each have a family, whether consanguine or adoptive, but when it comes to marriage possibilities we've a number of workable partners to choose from, and it's up to us to be discerning enough to select a mate who best suits us and our family structure, if we hope to have relationships with as much happiness and harmony as possible.

The editor quickly accepted the story and said, "Young girls need to know that it's not flattering when a boyfriend is overly jealous; it's a sign of danger. Your heroine's experiences prove that in how her boyfriend tried to destroy her family so he could have her all to himself. But the outcome was that he ended up destroying her love. Young girls need to realize that this is what jealousy does to relationships."

This particular story was multi-themed, but other confessions that are also very entertaining may have themes that seem pedestrian by comparison.

Good triumphing over evil was the theme for my story, "I Was a Hand-Me-Down Wife," which also bore out the ideology that nice guys don't always finish last.

In this story there were two orphaned brothers as different as day and night. The heroine—the narrator of the story—was involved with the blackguard, and when he was sent off to prison, the decent brother stepped in to provide for the disillusioned young girl who was left alone and found herself pregnant. All along the decent brother had been scorned by his wild brother, portrayed as a boring goody-two-shoes, but because she has few options the girl moves in with him, secretly considering the young man something of a chump. But she needs shelter so she is agreeable to becoming his housekeeper in exchange for a place to live. Over the course of time a relationship of mutual need—platonic, but deep—occurs, and eventually the heroine realizes what substance there is to the righteous brother who treats her so kindly, is always thoughtful, and performs like a father for her child born of another man. Still clinging to girlish dreams, however, instead of acknowledging reality, she awaits the other brother's release from prison. But true to nature, always brash and acting before he thinks, the blackguard brother breaks out of prison, causing the situation to go from bad to worse as he becomes a hunted man. When the authorities warn the very moral fellow of his brother's escape, and assure him they'll try to avoid a shoot-out, he fears that the dashing renegade he believes the girl still loves will come for her, she'll leave with him, and he'll lose the only girl he's ever cared about. The woman, who's blossomed in his care and knows what it's like to feel secure and loved, has come to have a sense of appreciation for what a *true man* is really like. When the escaped convict comes to claim his one-time playmate—who has since matured—she's faced with choosing between the two brothers. The good man triumphs over the evil fellow as the woman he loves stands by him, risking her life to save him. The convict is captured and the couple, who've come to acknowledge their love, head off to obtain a marriage license to make their arrangement legal, and move their relationship beyond the bonds of platonic love to full expression.

How your story characters will arrive at decisions, how they will grow from their choices, and what they will learn from their experiences will bear out the theme—and provide the take-away message that you will share with your readers as you craft stories to convincingly "argue" philosophies that you believe are universal truths worth sharing.

Once you select the theme, you can set about isolating the basic conflict, choose the most unpredictable cause-and-effect plot elements, and then mold the individual characters you'll need to make your stories "work."

CHAPTER
4

Compiling Conflicts Within the Confession Story

4.1 What Is Conflict?

Simply put, a conflict is an obstacle standing between a main character and easy realization of his or her goal in life.

The conflict, which can be either internal or external, or a combination of both, must be a difficulty of such severity that it's not possible for the narrator to "ignore it in hopes that it'll go away." It must be of such scope that the narrator is forced to take action, even if loath to do so, because inaction will most certainly cause the circumstances to go from bad to worse.

4.2 Where to Find Sources for Conflict

In the realm of fiction writing there are specific conflict "formulas" because almost any problem any character will ever face, be it in short stories or in novels, can generally be categorized in one of the several areas of conflict. These are:

Man against man.
Man against nature.
Man against himself.
Man against environment.
Man against machine.

4.3 Conflict Types Common in the Confession Story

In the confession field, the most frequent forms of conflict are "man against himself," "man against environment," and "man against man."

"Man against machine"-type stories tend to be concentrated in the horror genre, although given the right slant it might be possible to develop a workable idea for the confession market if it's handled appropriately.

Frequently man against nature conflicts arise in confessions, and I have used them many times, but in my stories if a flood, tornado, dangerous rodeo bucking horse, earthquake, or rabid dog are a source of duress, it's usually in the form of a supporting problem which may serve as the catalyst for the major man against man, man against himself, or man against environment conflict.

Changes in environment create new situations, and they give rise to myriad problems that the general population can relate to as readers recall how events may have drastically altered day-to-day routines in their own lives. Thus, they understand sudden stress thrust upon confession characters.

We all have our comfortable little niches. Story people are no different. We know that if our normal environment is altered, or if our personal sense of prestige in the family, community, or love relationship suffers a radical change, as a result we are placed in conflict.

The narrator in my story, "Why Is Everyone Blaming Me For My Boyfriend's Death?" printed in *Black Confessions* published by Lexington Library Inc., is a girl, Kendra Jones, who finds her environment radically changed by external forces:

> The night was tenderly balmy—a perfect evening for a big spring dance. I felt kissed by magic as Aunt Margie primped and fussed with my hair and makeup.
>
> "You're pretty as a picture, baby," she said. "How I wish your mama and daddy could see you now."
>
> I swallowed at the lump in my throat. "Me, too," I whispered.
>
> Although it had been a year already, it felt at times as if it had been only the day before when they'd been coming home from a company party given for the sales reps, and a drunk driver broad-

sided our stationwagon, killing my parents and my brother, Ted, who they'd picked up after his ball game.

Thank God that Aunt Margie and Uncle Melvin were there to take over and take me in. Without them I couldn't have faced living when all I wanted to do was fall down on the three freshly mounded graves covered with wilting flowers and die, too.

But Margie and Melvin convinced me that there was still plenty to live for, and they stressed that the best way I could show my love and respect for my parents was by being the kind of girl they'd always wanted me to become. A girl who studied hard and made good grades. A girl with her eye on the future, with plans to get educated and really become a somebody who could make a difference in the world. And a good girl who'd remain chaste like they had raised me—a young woman with plans to wait for the right man—and when I got married, have it all. A husband who adored me, with kids we could be proud to present to the world.

But it wasn't easy always doing the right thing, and to continue to place value on my goals. Believe me it wasn't easy . . . especially when the kids would call me a grind because I always studied so hard. . . .

The change in her environment presents her with conflicts, due to the deaths of her parents, that she might not have experienced to such a degree had the family not met with tragedy. As it is, any natural teenage stress over moral decisions is intensified. Because Kendra wants to honor her mother's and father's memory and be the kind of girl she knows they'd have wanted her to become, that means she can't do what might be tempting, or "in," otherwise she'd feel she was not only disappointing them but letting herself down as well.

4.4   Conflicts from Within and Without

Conflicts can originate internally or externally. They can be circumstances that could be within the narrator's control if she was strong enough or savvy enough to realize it. Or they can be situations beyond the character's control because others sometimes hold unpleasant sway over her life, with her left to cope with resulting conflicts just the same. There are times when others, by their actions, give her no choice but to react.

That's what causes the heroine of "Fantasy Lover," published by

Bronze Thrills, one of Lexington Library's magazines, to open up a resale shop in her home. The source of conflict—a jealous husband who doesn't want his wife to work, when she very much wants a career of her own—sets the stage for her to find a solution when she opens an in-home business.

Rolly was getting ready to go to work, and I whisked my fingers over the ziplock sandwich bag, tossed it into his lunchpail, flicked the clasps into place, and turned like a robot to have him drop a kiss across my lips as he snatched the lunchbucket from my hands. Our habitual, almost mechanical, morning routine was disrupted when the telephone shrilled.

"Who the hell is that?" Rolly asked, frowning.

Although I'd never, never cheated on him—and hadn't even given it a thought—my husband was as jealous as he could be.

"Probably a wrong number," I said in a blithe tone.

"Yeah. Right." Rolly shot me a suspicious glance and dropped his lunchpail onto the counter with a bang and scooped the receiver off the hook himself, growling into it. He listened a moment then contritely handed it to me. "It's your mother. . . ."

"Hi, Mama," I said, plopping onto the kitchen stool as I poured myself what was left in the coffee pot as Rolly went out the door.

"What's the matter with that man of yours?" she asked. "He sure sounds cranky this morning."

"Oh, nothing," I said, as I fluffed my shoulder length hair. "You know how he is. Rolly won't trust me to go to work. But he doesn't trust me when I'm staying at home, either . . . And we could sure use a second income. I wish I could find a way to earn some money without leaving home. . . ."

4.5   When to Introduce the Source of Conflict

Confession editors always want the problem in a story delineated as soon as possible, in the very opening paragraphs if it can be done. They expect the conflict to be isolated for the reader certainly no later than within the first five hundred words because neither editors nor readers want to wade through page after page of prose to figure out what's going on and where the action is leading.

In my story, "Teenage Sexpot Stepmother—My Stepson Sold My Intimate Poses to His Friends," another story acquired by Lexington

Library, Inc., the basic situation and source of conflict are presented
to the reader beginning with the first sentence.

"Happy Birthday to me, Happy Birthday to me, Happy Birthday
dear Stanley, Happy Birthday to me—"

I couldn't help laughing as my thirty-two-year-old husband
serenaded himself in the shower just off the master bedroom in the
home we shared with his two kids from his first marriage, twelve-
year-old Andrew, and nine-year-old Megan, whose mother had
died two years earlier from unexpected complications arising after
routine surgery.

Stan gave me a pinch on the bottom as he entered the kitchen.

"You're chipper today," I observed.

He grinned. "They say you're as old as you feel. And today I've
got the constitution—and desires—of an eighteen-year-old
dude."

I rolled my eyes. "Women and children, get off of the streets," I
warned, " 'Cause here comes Stan my Man."

"Maybe it's because the kids aren't around that I feel like one
again myself."

"Could be."

It really was nice having them off at camp. It was less stressful.
Meg, I got along with fine. Andy? Well . . . that was a different
story altogether.

"So what're we going to do for your birthday?"

"What've you got in mind?"

"It's your big day, Tiger, so you decide. I'll go along with
whatever you choose."

Stan's eyes widened. "Is that a promise?"

"Sure, Handsome, whatever you want to do, we do it."

"Is that a promise?" he repeated.

"What do you mean by that? Have I ever gone back on my word
to you?"

"No . . . but I have something really special in mind. And I
don't want to go to the trouble and expense if you're going to
chicken out on me."

"I told you, Stan, it's your birthday. When I turn twenty, then
it'll be my turn to be Queen for a Day."

"Princess," he said, grinning slowly, "you've got a deal." He
extended his hand for us to "shake on it." "When I get home,

darlin', be ready to draw the drapes and celebrate like you've never celebrated before."

The narrator is not expecting it when her husband returns home with a rented cam-corder, blank video cassettes, and—reminding her she'd given her solemn word to do his bidding—tells her that they're going to film themselves making love. Even though she's reluctant, she realizes that she did give him her word so she goes along with it against her better judgment.

4.6   Choosing a Conflict to Make Readers Care

In a confession story, whatever the problem you select, the conflict must be so serious that the reader will instinctively feel compassion for another person in such straits, and experience sympathy to the degree that the reader can condone a narrator when she takes action, even if what she attempts may be morally wrong, because the reader will feel there have been extenuating circumstances that "drove" the character to such behavior.

Desperate people do desperate things, and that's how the narrator felt in "Phone Sex," published in *Black Secrets*, another Lexington Library, Inc., title. The girl's overly protective mother does not allow her a social life, so the lonely young woman creates her own romantic life with the assistance of Ma Bell.

The story opens with her circumstances being sketched in for the readers' benefit so they'll know "where she's coming from":

I'd made up my mind. I was a freshman in high school, just past fifteen, and I was determined that Mama was going to stop treating me like I was still in kindergarten.

As I waited for her to get home from work, I paced the floor in our neat, modest apartment in a clean neighborhood. Nervously I wrung my hands. I was really stressed out. But I was also very, very determined.

"Mama," I began my rehearsed words the instant she walked through the door, momentarily staggering under the weight of the sack of groceries she'd carried from the corner Mom and Pop store. "I've got to talk to you. It's really important."

I followed her into the kitchenette. She thunked the sack onto the table and gave a weary sigh. She hung her coat away, seeming distracted, maybe a bit more tense than usual, but I plunged ahead anyway, before my courage could depart.

"Mama, I am past fifteen. I get good grades. I make the high honors roll. I'm dependable. I do what chores you specify. Therefore, I really think that I'm old enough so that you should let me go out with boys sometimes, and—"

When I saw Mama's dark brows fork into a frown, I knew that I should've known better than to try to talk to her after a rough day on the job. She was in no mood to restructure our—my—life.

At work I know that Mom's a whiz at negotiations. But at home she could be really rigid and unyielding. Especially when the topic was my permission to start dating. Her mother hadn't cared what Mama did, so long as she stayed out of her way when she did it. As a result, Mama became pregnant with me when she was little more than a child herself. Maybe Mama's mother cared too little—but couldn't Mama see that maybe she cared too much?

4.7   Use Conflict to Generate Sympathy

It is essential that the reader feel understanding for the narrator and be willing to forgive her poor choices, which I believe is the case, when the girl isn't allowed any increased social privileges. As a result, when her mother works overtime the girl gets on the phone and has a secret and anonymous romantic life. Her mother knows nothing about it until a representative of the telephone company contacts her after a boy's mother reports bothersome calls to the telephone company. Sophisticated equipment is used, and the girl was caught in an embarrassing trap. The mortified mother then has to reconsider her rigid thinking and it results in a better family environment to allow the girl room to grow and mature naturally.

As the story progresses the tension over the conflict should be such that each time the narrator is defeated—as is necessary to heighten suspense and create a riveting plot—the reader should feel the sting of setback, too.

Bringing in plot action that results in the narrator facing humiliation, tragedy, bad luck, hurt feelings, loss, etcetera, can allow the reader to relate to the narrator on an emotional level and continue to like her even when she makes seriously flawed choices, which the reader will feel might be justified, or at least understandable, given such stressful circumstances.

The narrator of "Teenage Sexpot Stepmother" feels it was a mistake to shoot the intimate footage on Stan's birthday, and several times she tries to "undo" that mistake, but her efforts are stymied when she and her husband are put into conflict with each other.

> "No way!" Stan protested. "Those videos are ours. MINE! They were your private birthday gift to me, remember? It was a fluke that Andy was looking for tapes in our bedroom. He doesn't rummage through my stuff very often. I'll bet he didn't even notice those tapes."
>
> "I suppose you're right," I reluctantly agreed.

In the next scene the conflict intensifies even further when the heroine discovers that the tapes are gone. Stan is out of town. When he phones home, she inquires if he took the tapes with him, and when he says that he didn't, horror descends upon her for she realizes that the tapes have fallen into the wrong hands.

> When Andrew came home I looked at him anew, trying to detect if there was something different about him. If maybe he'd seen his own father making love to an attractive, younger woman.
>
> Instead of a guilty expression, I saw his expensive running shoes. The jewelry. The costly jacket. I knew Stan gave the kids money for clothes, and I used his charge card when I shopped for them myself. But I knew we hadn't bought items in that price range.
>
> My stomach rolled over. How had a twelve-year-old boy obtained that kind of money? Was he dealing drugs? Or was he distributing homemade pornography?

4.8   The Importance of Writing About Appealing People in Conflict

Always keep in mind that if you, as the writer, can't find it within yourself to like and sympathize with your narrator, don't expect editors and readers to. And once you get reader sympathy, don't take it for granted, for you must work to keep it, for no matter how enticing your opening paragraphs, how unpredictable and exciting the ending, how clever and well-paced the mid-section is, the writer's effort goes for nought if the narrator loses reader sympathy. A good way to win reader sympathy is to make the narrator seem just a little different, in ways we've all felt self-conscious about at one time or another. For instance:

It was July hot, not a whisper of a breeze, and a sweat bee was buzzing around my face, but I didn't dare swat at it for fear that the auctioneer crying the estate sale twenty miles from the Texas city where I had my antique shop would think that I was upping the bid.

Beside me the boxes of what others considered plunder, and I knew to be treasures from another era piled higher and odds and ends of collectibles, that come Monday morning would have shelf space in my shop with neat price tags affixed.

In my linen dress and pastel summer shoes that matched my handbag, I stuck out like a sore thumb as I was surrounded by wind-burned ranchers in faded denims and their wives in easy care housedresses, shorts, breezy culottes, or jeans. Too late I was wishing I'd had the sense to dress like one of them.

I had scarcely passed a word with anyone all day long—except for the auctioneer—although they were friendly when I met someone's eyes and we exchanged smiles. I knew that they were aware of who I was; they considered me "the antique lady." I was also privy to the fact that a number of times people who'd had no real interest in an item jumped in just to run up the price so that the city slicker antiques lady wouldn't get a homespun country treasure too inexpensively.

I didn't know how I was going to get all of my items to my van, and I hesitated to ask a favor, although I sensed that they'd be offended if I offered to hire someone's services as could so easily be done in the city.

I was so busy wool-gathering as I planned my life for the next few hours that I almost missed it when the auctioneer's assistant held up a set of salt and pepper shakers, a popular design forty years earlier, but of limited production.

"Over here!" I cried, waving as I hastily cast my bid, knowing that one of my customers who'd been on the lookout for just such a set, would be elated.

I hadn't expected much competition—not even from the seller's neighbors or relatives who'd been upping the bid—after all, you had to really know your antiques to be aware of which salt and pepper sets were worth a pricey sum, and which were not.

What I certainly had not anticipated was to have a new face enter the bidding arena. During the afternoon I'd spotted those in the crowd for the sole purpose of running up the bids. But one glance into this man's face—what a face it was!—and I knew he was not one of them. For a moment I helplessly stared and didn't even hear the auctioneer's patter, but managed to somehow nod as expected to keep the price climbing each time I was outbid.

Beneath a Stetson and wrap-around sunglasses, was a sensual mouth, a toothpick tucked in the corner, perfectly displaying a beautifully clefted chin. And like a bonus thrown in, when the fellow threw a smile to an acquaintance standing nearby, dimples winked. As if that wasn't enough, he was bare-chested, with old military dog tags resting on his lightly furred skin.

For some reason, I continued to bid, even beyond the point that would allow me a profit. Cowboy pulled out his wallet, looked in, and asked the auctioneer if he took credit cards. The audience roared with good-natured laughter.

"Not the plastic, buddy," the auctioneer said. "But we'll take a cash-advance credit card check. Got yours along?"

"Just a minute," the fellow said. His search seemed to take forever. "Here they are!" he triumphantly announced, producing his credit card cash advance checks that had been folded and carried in his wallet until they were battered. "I'm still in."

"Oh, let him have them if he wants them that much," I said, laughing, feeling my features flush as eyes flicked toward me. "It's not worth it."

As the sale began to wind down people trickled away. With a strange mix of emotions I was both relieved and piqued that the handsome cowboy remained, but I was glad that the crowds had thinned as it would afford me less of a problem in getting my van negotiated close enough to get my purchases loaded so I could head for home.

"You here all alone, Ma'am?" a deep voice asked when the auctioneer offered the last item and the crowd dispersed.

I glanced up. It was him!

"Oh, why, yes. Yes, I am," I said.

"You'll need some help, then." He didn't pose it as a question, he stated it as a fact, and in the process, unspoken, offered his services.

"Th-that would be wonderful."

"Where's your rig parked?"

"My van's down the road a little ways," I said. "It was the closest I could park when I arrived."

"There was a dandy crowd, wasn't there? If you'll trust me with your keys, I could bring your van up here and help you load 'er up."

Trust him with my keys? At that moment I was ready to trust him with my heart!

Once you select an idea, develop a theme, pinpoint the basic problem, and consider ways to maintain the conflict, it will result in the plotting being made easy as you maneuver the necessary elements into the best possible order, then link them together to create a unified, satisfying confession story.

CHAPTER
5

Plotting the Confession Story

5.1   What Is a Plot?

Essentially the plot is the logical start-to-finish, cause-and-effect sequence that links action and comprises the structural unity that makes the story entertaining when experienced as a whole.

In something like a domino effect, for in any well-plotted story one incident occurs, and when it takes place that serves as the catalyst to make something else happen. Which in turn results in another situation transpiring, which sets another action into motion until at some point the combination of events reaches a "climax," make-or-break aspect, and the resolution arrives, with the story quickly drawing to a close thereafter.

The plot is the cause-and-effect relationship of a character facing a specific conflict to resolve, with the ideal solution arising out of that character's unique background and personality traits.

5.2   Which Comes First—People or Plot?

So which comes first, the character or the plot?

Frequently they arrive together. Plotting is a carefully balanced undertaking with the author objectively judging the possibilities, adding a bit here, taking away there, slightly rearranging someplace else, to fine-tune the story's skeleton so that it's a full-bodied piece surrounding "flesh and blood characters" so that the combined elements create a memorable plot.

To be technical, the plot probably always arrives first, by way of the idea that catches the fancy of a writer who considers what kind of theme can be proven by developing the premise. This results in isolating a conflict to use as a jumping off point to use to enter the action and begin that particular story.

This creative process, which may take place with almost computer-like speed, allows the author to consider and reject a spate of possibilities until only one or two solid story lines remain. It then hinges on a character to make a specific idea work—as certain aspects need to be carefully shaped to make what otherwise might not be believable seem not only credible, but because of background, wholly plausible—for that individual.

In the confession story, plot and people (the conflict episodes and characters), while they are separate elements, are as linked as Siamese twins. Where you find one you'll also locate the other, and editors are equally concerned with the viability of both.

When buying stories for their magazines, confession editors constantly consider the backgrounds of their average readers, and analyze how they will react to your story's plot and people.

Here are some typical comments made by editors:

"The plot is thin, familiar, and way too predictable. Plus, the narrator is not sympathetic. Readers won't root for her."

"This story is capably written, but it's mind-boggling in its twists and turns, and as a result isn't entirely believable. The narrator seems more caught up in life than involved in creating her own fate through the strength of her choices."

"This story is very well-written but it's difficult to follow. Too much happens in this to make it readable. It is tricky enough so that it would not be easily followed or understood by our average reader, who would, however, probably really like and identify with this heroine. If you can simplify the plot—please try me again."

"This is interesting, but there's no serious conflict for the narrator in this, and as a result the plot is lacking. Sorry that we have to pass it up."

These editorial comments sum up most confession editors' requirements: there should be enough plot . . . but not too much.

5.3   Taking the Pain out of Plotting

Because plotting can be a drawn-out process, and for a beginner, a frustrating, even frightening experience, you can accomplish it with less agony if you do it when you're away from the keyboard. Sitting before a blank sheet of paper, or staring at a blinking cursor, can make the plotting process seem unduly formidable. It is much easier to map out a story in your mind while driving to work, doing the dishes, mowing the grass, vacuuming the carpet, or performing simple chores that do not require a great deal of concentration.

A notebook and pen kept in a strategic place will suffice for jotting down possibilities, and for those who're very mobile, a portable micro-cassette recorder can be a wonderful work aid allowing you to preserve your audio notes when you're unable to safely jot reminders in a notebook.

Whichever method you chose, I urge you to take time to enter your ideas and plot considerations somewhere that allows you to return to them for easy referral.

Do not try to keep it all in your head, because even authors with exceptionally good memories have learned the hard way that the memory-alone system is destined for failure when the idea that seemed so brilliant and unforgettable (that the writer believed he or she would never have trouble recalling it) totally departs except for the author's remembering that the idea was one of unforgettable quality!

No one has come up with exacting rules for plotting, although for many years there have been plot wheels, story charts, and now computer programs that are reported to help authors cope with what is for some a difficult task, for others an easy mental undertaking, but at the same time a somewhat ethereal act which most authors find themselves incapable of explaining to others in concrete, definitive terms.

5.4 Common Patterns for Plotting

A "formula" helps authors to give their ideas direction as they plot a story, so they can make a conscious effort to include what aspects manuscripts in the field are expected to contain.

In the confession field, since the earliest days of the pulp magazines back in the 1920's, the confession story "formula" has been "sin-suffer-and-repent." Even today that literary pattern is as valid as it was back then, and this gives a confession writer a standard blueprint to use when building a story from the ground up.

Almost every confession story that's published is in some way or another shaped along the lines of sin-suffer-and-repent. The basic differences arise, depending on which sin-suffer-and-repent aspect has been accented, and which element, by comparison, has been given a lighter treatment because usually the components are not stressed equally.

In confession stories we always know that the reader is going to "sin"—make a mistake (or be made to feel as if she's made a mistake).

We know that the confession narrator will "suffer." She's made miserable through her own erroneous actions, or at the hands of those who have jumped to conclusions and believe her situation to be something that it's not, or who don't understand her, or refuse to accept her for some reason, and as a result she's unfairly persecuted. Regardless of its origin, suffer she does.

We also know that there will be someone in the story who is going to "repent," whether it's the heroine who recognizes her errors, or those who've shabbily treated our narrator and have become aware of their mistaken ways and seek her forgiveness. And after repentance will come the serenity and peaceful co-existence that everyone wants.

5.5 Making Plot Variables Add Up to an Exciting Story

Once the writer has selected an idea and considered the theme (which is dictated by preferred outcome), then figured out the conflicts—that will hold sway over the character, who will in return dictate the story line—plotting is recognizably like working an algebra equation in which $w + ? + ? = z$.

So given several known quantities, and a list of variables, and by logically attaching them to a cause-and-effect factor to see if they add up, a writer can calculate the various plot possibilities that can create a sum that reveals itself as the right answer for that specific story's equation.

5.6 The Beginning + ? + the End = a Solid Plot Structure

In other words, when it comes to plotting, if you know the beginning and are aware of how you want the story to end, you can calculate your way through to find the middle.

Usually the beginning of a story arrives first, and you can start the plot there.

As has already been discussed, it may be sparked by an idea you've seen mentioned in the news, a remark overheard, or a situation addressed in an advice column.

You already know the basic premise to begin the story. So you must identify the conflict for the reader when you introduce the character. You may also choose to make a bid for sympathy. But before you can begin writing with surety, and go beyond the first scene, you'll need to have a sense of direction. So you must choose your destination, the story's end.

At that point you should begin to move steadily toward that objective, taking the most direct route available but also one that's a "scenic route" in that, figuratively speaking, it's got valleys, mountaintops, boulevards, and wilderness trails. This will present a "surprise around every corner" for the reader and keep the audience involved in the story, constantly wondering what will happen next.

5.7 How It's Done

Here's an example of the mental processes when I plotted an idea and developed it into a successful confession story, jotting in my notebook the working title "The High Cost of Living Taught Us the High Cost of Loving" after scanning *Playboy*, where I read an article about a happily married man, "Fearless Fred," who had an unusual way of bringing home the bacon. Fearless Fred, who'd become unemployed due to an economic recession, worked as a male prostitute.

Fred, a heterosexual, didn't cruise the streets, indiscriminately soliciting business. Instead, he drove a small van outfitted with various specialized equipment, and he set up appointments to satisfy the needs of the frustrated women who could afford to hire his expert services.

It was certainly an unusual occupation. But what I found most noteworthy about the situation was that Fred's wife knew about his endeavor and was supportive of his new and very profitable business venture.

Interesting people, I thought. Incredible situation, I decided. But what could happen if his wife didn't know, I speculated.

And in that consideration, I saw the beginnings of a confession story.

The beginning: A man is going to work as a male prostitute.

The ending: A woman is going to make an appointment to be serviced by a male prostitute, and the shocking conclusion will be when she discovers that she knows the man who shows up to keep the appointment!

To get started: For a submission title I selected, "I Hired a Man to Love Me," because I wanted the story from the woman's point of view, since the chances to sell a story are better from the female point-of-view rather than from a man's.

With the surprise ending the startling revelation that the male hooker is someone known to the narrator, it seemed to me that a single woman—one who is shy, or homely, or desperately desiring some romantic experience—hiring a man for thrills could be dramatic.

But hey! It would be even more dangerous and potentially dramatic if it were a married woman paying for such unorthodox services.

Therefore, I selected for my narrator a character who would be a wife, and to help readers relate to her, I also decided that she would be a mother of children, with them of sufficient age so that they're independent and don't come into play within the story to clutter up the action and get in the way of the plot.

The problem: She has a sudden conflict in her life because her sex life has gone from being dynamite to, putting it kindly, disappointing. It's so bad, in fact, that she's going to look for relief elsewhere if there isn't some improvement soon.

To keep all-important reader sympathy, however, the narrator will need a very compelling reason to do something like seek satisfaction in the arms of another man. Divorce? It's out. She can't afford it. And anyway, she really loves the guy, the father of her children, and until recently he was a lover of such tender dimension that there'd been no room for improvement.

In the reality I assigned to her, this very nice lady is married to a fellow who's a pretty good guy, so there has to be extenuating circumstances, and that means that she can't simply go looking for thrills right away. She stews about her problem, she hopes it'll go away as magically as it appeared, but plot circumstances can't allow this, so she must face obstacles that "tighten the screws" even more.

At this point I focused on some basic questions:

Why?

What?

How?

Why wasn't the narrator enjoying a satisfying intimate relationship at home? The answer: Because her husband is suddenly disinterested in sex, and claims that he's too exhausted by the long hours required by his new job as a salesman (employment she knows he doesn't enjoy, but took after being laid off at his former workplace before he could qualify for unemployment benefits).

What happens when a husband ignores his wife's physical needs? She becomes frustrated. She starts to feel unloved. She begins to question her womanly appeal. Her self-image and confidence are damaged.

How long will the narrator put up with it? Probably only as long as it takes her to realize that she has a problem, and then is driven to take action to find a solution to the dilemma.

How will she do it? Initially she'll attempt in-home projects of the nature that readers themselves, faced with the same conflict, would choose to pursue. The heroine is planning for success (while the behind-the-scenes author is dispassionately plotting her downfall).

In "I Hired a Man to Love Me," the heroine plans a romantic seduction of her husband.

What makes the situation go from bad to worse? Despite her good intentions and commendable efforts, the romantic interlude bombs when her husband is unable to perform, then falls asleep, snoring in her ear, and she's hurt, frustrated, and suddenly desperate to prove to herself that she's not so unappealing and boring that no man, not even her husband, can get enthused about making love to her.

Then *what* does she do? For the moment, nothing. She can't bring herself to have an affair, for she's not that kind of woman, but she would enjoy a bit of lovemaking, and what she'd savor even more is the affirmative knowledge that a virile man finds her attractive and is helpless not to respond to her.

How would the idea of retaining a hired lover come to a rather unsophisticated wife and mother as a possible solution? As the author I analyzed ways that the purveyors of sex reach their targeted audience. The woman is a homebody, she doesn't frequent bars, she'd be uncomfortable going into a singles' lounge, she's not likely to get picked up on the street, so that means that the information must be, literally, dropped into her very lap.

Knowing what I needed, I gave her a hobby that due to the cost of postage, and bills from when her husband was laid off, she feels she can no longer afford: sweepstaking/contesting. Because of past efforts my narrator is now on almost every mailing list in the Western world, and her letter carrier delivers an armload of "junk" mail almost every day.

One afternoon her next door neighbor drops in for coffee, is glancing through a sample copy of a regional tabloid, and she begins reading the "personals" advertisements in the back pages. Giggling, she wonders what woman would ever be so desperate for thrills that she'd hire a male prostitute to make love to her.

The heroine grabs the paper, reads the ad, joins in the laughter, but in that instant the idea is planted.

To retain reader sympathy, however, the narrator can't race to the telephone, tap in the number, make an appointment and rush from her house to rendezvous with the man. The reader would never go along with that. Not yet. The woman must try again to rekindle the spark in her marriage. And to keep sympathy, only when she's rebuffed or humiliated, can desperation drive her to make a date, an act that the reader can now understand, accept, and even sympathize with.

The narrator immediately plans a candlelight dinner with plenty of wine. The kids are conveniently away at summer camp (that they can now afford again) and the narrator sets the scene for another attempt at seduction.

Of course, because the plot requires it, the effort fails as miserably as her earlier attempt and she's even more hurt and humiliated.

The next day, feeling she has nothing to lose, and her self-esteem to regain, she gives in during a weak moment and makes an appointment with a hired lover.

At the appointed hour she goes to the hotel room, but as she awaits the man's arrival she's full of self-recrimination as she considers her poor, tired husband, slaving away at that very moment to provide for her and the kids, working at a job she knows he hates because he never talks about it, while she's blithely getting ready to revel away the afternoon with another man, using money her husband—who's always been a good provider—has earned to pay another man to make love to her.

The readership is nodding along; that's probably what they, too, would be thinking about were they in her predicament.

What does she decide? In a self-righteous frame of mind the narrator realizes that she'd better go home, face the problem, and talk it out with her husband before a rash action she'll regret will make things even worse. She believes that with communication paving the way they can settle their differences and find a workable solution, and maybe even discuss the possibility of him switching to a line of work that he won't find so exhausting and unfulfilling.

But the heroine—who has just experienced her moment of truth—is rushing to leave the hotel room after "seeing the light" in her come-to-realize scene, when the story's climax takes place.

Her husband barges in the open door she's exiting from, they collide, stare at each other, and realize the sordid, shattering truth: he's a male prostitute and she's a woman desperate enough to require his services.

All the actions, character traits, and imparting of background information for credibility have led to this moment with the spouses facing each other. For the reader it should be quite unexpected, but also perfectly logical, made believable because all the vital data had been presented to the reader as the story progressed.

During the plotting of this story—starting with a man who was going to work as a hooker and ending with the fact that some woman was going to recognize him—I considered many possibilities. Some were very good, some were not, but all variables paled when compared to having it be not just "any man" and not just "any woman," but characters who, because they were husband and wife, gave major urgency to the overall plot.

From the plot arose their necessary character traits. But from their character traits also came their personalized plot line.

5.8   More How to Do It

As another plotting example, when I saw the *Time* magazine article about couples who rented video cameras and made home videos of themselves making love, I knew that I had a dynamite idea.

The beginning—my premise—was going to be a couple who rented equipment and made their own in-home blue movie.

As a person with respect for what can happen when letters,

diaries, pictures, etcetera fall into the wrong hands, I shuddered over what possible tragedies could result from erotic home videos being viewed by people not meant to see them.

I had my plot beginning.

Now I needed some characters. And I had to shape them to best plot the story. Their conflict was going to be that he was gung ho for the idea, but she was reticent. He thought it was a nifty idea. She felt it was potentially dangerous. The end result would be—just as she feared—that the wrong hands would gain possession of their filmed escapades.

Necessary story elements required that I shape my characters to perfectly suit the story—and shape the story to fit the characters.

Who is most likely to feel comfortable taking their own intimate movies while making love? A married couple.

What risks were they running in doing so? Whose "wrong hands" were the videotapes most likely to fall into? Their children's, because kids so often tend to be the video aficionados in most households. And with such a betrayal it's probably going to be a son, not a daughter, because I'd read statistics that men think about sexual topics with far more frequency than do females.

At that point, my title was born: "My Son Sold My Intimate Poses to His Curious Friends."

Provocative, I decided, but . . . not terribly realistic. I sensed that most sons, if they discovered a video of their consanguine father and mother making love, might watch the action, but then out of a sense of family loyalty would do nothing more with the damaging film.

For my story's purposes I needed a son who didn't care what happened to his mother.

So the working title was edited accordingly—and the family relationships evolved in a different direction. It became: "My Stepson Sold My Intimate Poses to His Curious Friends."

Frequently, I realized, stepchildren don't accept a new stepmother, and therefore, if a boy resented his young stepmother and found a porno movie starring her and his father, the bonds of loyalty would not be there, so he'd have no compunction about letting his friends see the homemade porno flick starring his old man with his new bimbo wife.

After mulling over the situation, I focused on the family unit, making necessary character and plot selections to shape the action and make the story work.

The husband, I realized, should be an older man, so he'd have teenage children. For sympathy's sake I decided he'd be a widower. His first wife died unexpectedly. Now he'd found love again—and was "like a kid with a new toy"—and the son is disgruntled that their father has married a woman not much older than he is (which gives the unspoken idea that maybe the kid is attracted to his stepmother).

For her part, I compiled traits to form a character who hopes to peacefully co-exist with her children. A young romantic, she makes it her life's mission to make her husband happy, and therefore, when he wants for his birthday present her agreement to let him videotape them making love, she agrees, because she can't refuse him something that seems to mean so much to him.

Later on she has second thoughts. Her husband enjoys viewing the video, but the narrator worries about it. She tries to talk her husband into destroying the videotape, begs him to let her do it, but he replies that they're *his* tapes, that they were her birthday gift to him, and they'll stay where they are in their secret hiding place.

When her husband is away on an extended business trip, the narrator gets to missing him, she goes to get the tapes from their hiding place, and she discovers that they are gone!

When her husband calls, she's almost hysterical as she asks what he did with the videotapes. He's stunned that they are missing, immediately suspects his sullen, moody son and he vows that the boy had better have the right answers when he phones home later on to get to the bottom of the matter.

When the stepson comes home, the heroine sees him in a different light. She notices the costly running shoes, the expensive jacket, the jewelry, and she realizes that while her husband has always been generous, he hasn't given the kids that kind of money.

The son answers the phone that night when his father calls, and the heroine is in her bedroom, with the receiver pressed to her ear and the "mute" button activated so she can listen in. She learns that her stepson had taken the tape to amuse his friends, but one of them confiscated it from him, made duplicate copies, and begun selling them. The youth had given the stepson money to keep him quiet.

The young woman's husband is furious, and before hanging up he promises to take action with very harsh terms of punishment. Recognizing the boy's fear, the stepmother realizes she can use a bleak moment to forge a bright future and start fresh with the boy, with them belatedly bonding as mother-son.

She has a frank talk with him, admits she'd been hurt, but assures the child that she loves him and can forgive him, and that she'll intervene with his father (as any caring mother would). And as a family, she assures the reader in her closing narrative statements at story's end, they'll just hold their heads high, and live down the talk, knowing that there was no real shame in a husband and wife who loved one another and expressed it physically . . . in private . . . but that the shame was in the betrayal when an outsider went public with a very personal videotape of memories. The narrator's pay-off— the anticipated happy ending—occurs when the boy hugs the wise young woman and for the first time calls her "Mom."

> It was like a miracle, *the narrator concludes in this confession story,* for Stan was soon offered a job as a regional manager. That meant we'd be moving three states away, where we didn't know anyone, and no one knew us, so we could escape the stigma caused by our "sex-capades."
>
> The experience was painful, but we all learned from it.
>
> Stan and me as a loving couple.
>
> And Stan, the kids, and I, as a caring, committed family.

So look over your ideas, then get ready to map out your story as you labor to figure out the cause-and-event sequence that will uphold your theme, and dictate what kinds of characters you'll need to help you execute a wonderful plot that will result in your creating truly memorable people.

CHAPTER
6

Characterization: Creating
"Flesh and Blood" People

Characterization is a stumbling block for many beginning writers. Almost as bad as the rejection slips saying that the plot is too thin and weak are those that state:

"Your characters don't come across as real flesh-and-blood individuals."

"Your characters are cardboard."

"Breathe some life into your people!"

"Avoid stereotypes. Make your people real and unique, not just a 'type'."

Know that "real" characters are not born—they are carefully created.

6.1   Types of Traits

Confession characters are composites of traits that may be categorized as *universal, physical,* and *emotional.*

Universal. These traits include such human capacities as being able to think, cry, breathe, smell, touch, laugh, and all of the other natural emotions, reactions, and abilities that readers will assume your character possesses, unless the readership is informed otherwise. So unless a character is an amputee, blind, deaf, or has a disability that is integral to the plot, you can let the reader assume that your characters are invested with all of the common, universal traits, and their presence can go without mention.

Physical. These traits have to do with appearance—short or tall, homely or beautiful, swarthy or fair, graceful or awkward, plump or svelte.

Emotional. These are traits that I feel are the most important for confession writers to use in characterizing a person and giving him or her credibility. These capacities include the ability to experience and express anger, lust, jealousy, disdain, resentment, shame, guilt, pride, sorrow, and myriad other emotions. These deep feelings must be conveyed through dialogue, action, or introspective narration to give the depth and reality to your confession characters that they will need to become realistic story people.

6.2   Keeping the Audience in Mind as You Create a Composite

When imbuing characters with traits, it helps to keep your audience in mind when you start putting components together.

Most confession readers consider themselves average people, so that means that they tend to relate to persons who are also quite average. Therefore, regardless of whether I'm writing for the black confession magazines, or slanting toward the white confession audience, I prefer not to describe the characters using physical details, and that way the same story can be submitted to either market without editing in any required changes to make the skin, eye, and hair color fit the targeted audience.

Readers will not relate to a narrator who is described as too fat, too thin, too homely, or too beautiful—so this should be avoided—unless such a trait has direct bearing on the plot line of the story—and the tale won't work otherwise.

In my story, "Too Homely to Date—But Not to Rape," published by *True Romantic Confessions*, the narrator's problem is that she's a very plain girl.

> I'd always known that I was plain. Well, maybe not always. But I'd been aware of it since the summer ten years before when I was five and my cousin came to visit Gram for two weeks.
>
> Uncle Harley, Gram's bachelor brother, held Gerilynn on his lap and dunked sugar cookies in his coffee while she took dainty bites. Across the table I slouched in my chair, wiggling my toes in the holes of my tennis shoes, and slopped crumbs and milk on Gram's

red checked oilcloth that covered the old-fashioned claw-footed table.

Gram smiled and smoothed my tangled braids as she went by.

Uncle Harley tucked Gerilynn's blond sausage curls into place.

"Compared to this'un, Sis," he murmured, gesturing at Gerilynn, "that'un," his head jerked in my direction, "looks like seven miles o' mud roads."

"Shhhh!" Gram frowned. Uncle Harley chuckled.

"Some were meant to be pretty," he said philosophically, "and some weren't. One thing they've got in common is they're sweet little girls."

Maybe Uncle Harley didn't think a five year old could understand what he said, but I did. Even when he tweaked my nose, and produced pieces of gum for both Geri and me, I wanted to cry. I had never felt so ugly in my life. . . .

Because of comparisons and contrasts, the reader sees the picture the narrator has created, and understands perfectly why the character feels unattractive. The reader, because of Harley's thoughtless input, is prepared to accept the narrator's specifics regarding her physical drawbacks.

6.3 Using Characterization to Generate Reader Identification

In most confession stories, readers will relate to the narrator and her feelings. Because they identify with her—homely or not—they "live" the story vicariously as they read it, and subconsciously they will gladly transfer their own physical traits to the character who refers to herself with the common "I."

Readers come to feel that they know the narrator, and feel of her as a friend, not because of her flaxen hair, china blue eyes, perfect cheekbones, or darling dimples, but because of how she feels deep down inside, and what emotions she conveys to them, causing them to remember incidents when they felt the same.

Readers are down-to-earth people, at times a bit fickle, and a writer risks making the narrator seem vain—and therefore unsympathetic—if she comments on her own beautiful features. This must be carefully conveyed. If your character is a real looker, better to apply characterization by a third party:

"Suzanne!" Peggy Glidden cried, momentarily drowning out the hurdy-gurdy music on the midway. Her mouth dropped open. "Is it really you?" Before I got a chance to reply, she hugged me hard, squealing in delight at our chance encounter.

"Yes, it's me," I said, smiling. "So how have you been?"

Peggy piffled a dishpan hand, then ran it through her wilting hair. "You know how it is. Same old same old," she weakly joked, tugging her T-shirt down over her ballooning hips. "But I can see how you've been. Suzy, you're gorgeous. You always were a pretty girl, but tan as you are, trim as you are, and with your hair hanging halfway down to the pockets of your designer jeans, it's no wonder that heads are turning when you walk by."

I felt myself blush, even as I hoped the words were true. "You're sweet to say so," I murmured.

"Sweet? I'm eaten up with jealousy," she blurted, but linked her arm through mine. "Tell me your secrets." She glanced across the scruffy grass and littered carnival grounds to where her husband was occupied with their three children. "I could use a little help in the self-improvement department. . . . Hank's talking about the new secretary at work. In fact, he's talking about her a lot."

6.4 Character Description in First-Person Viewpoint—Narrator

A narrator referring to herself in that vein of being gorgeous would seem like an egomaniac. A supporting member of the story's cast (who is described, herself, by the heroine's impressions of her old friend) is a writing trick that allows both people to be described for the reader at once, and without seeming like the story line has taken time out to list off a set of vital statistics.

A character can describe herself by sharing with the reader narrative and dialogue explaining what she is not—rather than focusing on what she is:

"You—you're just like your mother!" Cal sputtered angrily. He hurled the words at me like rocks, and his face was ashen with fury. He shook his head in disgust, then stomped from the house, slamming the door behind him.

I felt deflated, like the wind had been knocked from me with the force of our fight.

I turned away from the back door, numb, and my tear-filled eyes caught my reflection in the sparkling clean window above the spotless sink, where the night outside was black as ink.

In the shiny pane I saw myself reflected: neat, clean, modestly dressed, pleasant-faced, with looks and a figure that were reasonably attractive.

I felt a spike of anger erupt. Then it ebbed and I was awash in hurt when Cal's words rang in my ears. More tears of hurt and confusion welled in my eyes to spill over and roll down my hot cheeks.

Had Cal said what he had simply because he knew that comparing me with Mom was guaranteed to cut to the quick? Or, was I blind to my own flaws? Was I really more like her than I ever wanted to admit?

The last time I'd accidentally run into Mom had been in town on main street almost three months before. She'd been blowsy and pale, her bleached hair matted. Her eyes were faded, red, and her makeup, which it looked like she'd applied with a trowel, couldn't begin to hide what she was, and offer silent testimony about the life she lived, flitting from bar to bar and man to man.

I considered how I'd worked so hard to leave my past behind, to be worthy to become Cal's wife. I'd spared no effort when it came to being a good mother to our children. I was a respected member of community organizations. I was a room mother at school. I was active at church. I wasn't like Mom—I was a decent person, dammit!

"I'm not like her," I whispered in a hollow tone. The words cracked on a sob. "You're wrong, Calvin Stephens," I muttered as I stared into the fathomless night and my lower lip trembled. "I'm not like my mother. And I never will be. I'll die before I make my children ashamed of me the way I've always been so ashamed of her. . . ."

In one brief scene the reader physically describes herself, she explains her background, she shares her goals in life, and via these emotions she forthrightly shares with the readers she becomes very "real" and even admirable.

6.5 Character Description in First-Person Viewpoint—By Others

There are times when the narrator fails to see herself as the rest of the world observes her, and it becomes necessary, then, to describe her more fully to the reader, and do it in such a way so that the reader, too, is suddenly startled by the true appearance of someone she might've assumed resembled herself.

This is what happened to the heroine, Aggie-Anne Carson, nick-named "Bubbles," the narrator of "Men Won't Marry a Tramp Like Me," published by *Intimate Story*.

A carnival worker, Aggie-Anne begins to dream that she has a future with Mark, a clean-cut rodeo rider she's been dating that summer while he follows the circuit to earn money for veterinary school and she works in a fast-food concession stand. A drunken cowboy's words dash her with nightmarish reality.

> I met my eyes in the filmy bathroom mirror over the basin in the tiny travel trailer. At that moment I saw what the drunken cowboy had seen. Me—with a bright red mouth and hardened eyes circled with too much makeup. My brassy blond hair was dark at the roots. I shook my head sadly. The drunken cowboy was right. I turned away with a sigh. We'd make some pair, all right, a tramp like me and Mark's sweet, prim, church-going little mama back in west Texas. . . .

Much of the time it's not necessary to physically describe the narra-tor. The man she loves, however, should be sketched in clearly, using any images that are appropriate to draw for the reader a mental portrait that will allow them to entertain romantic visions of him, too.

Myra, a wealthy rancher's daughter, in "Too Hot To Wait for the Right Man," published in *Intimate Story*, uses narrative to present a clear vision of what her love interest is like:

> Clete had changed from the wild and woolly rodeo bum he'd been when he came to the ranch five years before when he was twenty-two and I was going-on-thirteen. Since then, Clete had calmed down. Mellowed, I guess you could say. He seemed content to wear himself out working the ranch during the day, and staying up late

at night out in the bunkhouse reading, that is, when he wasn't playing checkers with me after supper.

Often I wondered about the bright lights, noise, and excitement of the big city and the people who followed the professional rodeo circuit as he'd done for several years.

But when I'd ask him to tell me what it was like, Clete would just smile slowly, and his gray eyes would grow distant. Then he'd change the subject. He never talked about it. But, the ornate silver championship belt buckle he wore, the trophies he had lined up on a shelf in the bunkhouse, and his slight limp, that got worse when he was really tired, were proof that Clete had been a top rider. He'd got out while the getting was good.

My heart pounded when I realized that Clete saw me in a different way, too. Lately he'd taken to treating me like . . . a woman, not a pain-in-the-neck kid.

6.6 Writing Techniques to Convey Characterizations

My heart skipped a beat when Clete towered over me, so tall and handsome with his sun-streaked brown hair that was striking against his coppery tan. His gunmetal gray eyes grew soft with love as he stared down at me. My body trembled with sudden confusion. I didn't know how to treat this new Clete, this Clete who was so unfamiliar to me. . . .

Characteristics can be revealed through dialogue, narration, introspection, comparison, contrast, or a combination of these methods, and present to the readership a well-rounded person who is a total personality.

Secondary characters may be described in some depth, or, to prevent the story from bogging down beneath too many details, glossed over. The other girl in the story "Phone Sex," published by *Black Secrets*, gets a quick treatment:

"Would you look at the sex kitten with Dace?" Jayne, my best friend whispered.

I did. I couldn't take my eyes off her. She was everything that I wanted to be and wasn't. She was slim, had beautiful posture, a gorgeous head of hair, a complexion that I'd have killed for, a darling nose, and pouting lips. She had sensual eyes and there was a regalness about her that seemed to signal that she felt herself every inch a queen—and the boys swarming around her were her willing subjects—ready to do her bidding.

6.7   Character Tags

Then again, supporting characters can be given a simple "tag" to help the reader keep them straight. This could be a nervous habit, unusual hair color, or some mannerism that will be associated with that person for the duration of the story.

6.8   Occupational Traits

Jobs and occupational references round out a story character, whether male or female. A clerk in a fashion boutique may be viewed as an avant-garde, bohemian trend-setter. A clerk in a bookstore may be considered to be more intellectual and quiet. A female clerk in a hardware store may be assumed automatically to be capable and self-sufficient, more so than her counterpart who is a clerk in a lingerie shop.

For men, jobs as a rodeo rider, electric lineman, lumberjack, wildcatting oilman, plainclothes policeman, race car driver, rancher, and other occupations that require strength and stamina may, without another word of description, hint at a character who is rugged and manly. Men who are librarians, pharmacists, bookkeepers, or secretaries, suggest a less visibly *macho* image.

6.9   Choosing Names to Characterize

Careful selection of your characters' names can help to highlight their possible personalities. Bubbles quickly presents a picture of a frivolous, voluptuous, scatterbrained sexpot. The name says it so well that you almost don't have to describe her. Names like Bunny, Cookie, Goldie, and citizens-band radio "handles," can also indicate a character type.

Names can give female characters an aura of glamor without a word of physical description, such as Kenna, Gayla, Krista, Shawna, Cricket, Jillian, Shannon, Karmen, Karyn—identities that are appropriate for lively young narrators. Ellen, Dorothy, Grace, Agnes, Alice, Frances, Louise, and Betty are names that may be viewed as a bit old-fashioned and tend to evoke the concept of a staid, reliable, sensible woman who would be able to offer comfort and logical advice to a troubled narrator.

For the men, rugged names can suggest a manly, competent, or romantic image like Clay, Derek, Guy, Frank, Ron, Rick, Roan, Jordan, Brett, Mitch, and Jared. On the other hand, names like Maurice, Horace, Cyril, Owen, Curtis, Gale, Doran, Lloyd or Henry, might suggest a less aggressive type.

A look through the telephone directory, or a book about naming babies, might provide many interesting first and last names. A name that's common in your area might be rarely used in another region of the nation.

You should avoid overusing the same names in stories, especially unusual names like Saranell, Caroldeen, Suebeth, or Lyndalu. A good way to prevent this is to keep a log of names that you have used in your stories. This can help you discover the beauty of names and how they can complement and add dimension to your characters' personality, while sparing the editor the quandary of having to rename your people if a number of stories she has recently acquired used the same common names.

It is also a good idea to keep a record of the occupations, particularly for the men, as this ensures that your stories will center around different and believable jobs. Attend a "Career Day" Exposition to pick up catalogs listing various opportunities, and make use of entrepreneurial publications that offer a bevy of ideas for characters who are self-employed. The story characters who are their own bosses are great to work with because you don't have to shape the action around their hours of employment.

By understanding your characters' universal, physical, and emotional traits, you can arrange for the people in your stories to become vibrantly alive on the page. And once they live on the page, let them take over and tell their stories, so that you, the author, serve as the conduit. With their personalities to guide you, they'll always remain "in character" and will transform mere "types" needed to make a specific story work into the flesh-and-blood people who will populate your stories and be loved and well-remembered by your readers.

CHAPTER
7

Technical Potpourri

7.1 Viewpoint

"Viewpoint" refers to the character through whom the story will be told. There are a number of different kinds of viewpoint, but in the confession story there is no leeway in which it can be used. Confession stories must be written from the first-person viewpoint because an individual can confess only to those things that she or he has done.

The first-person viewpoint makes use of the pronouns "I," "me" and "my" and as a result the reader experiences events from the main character's frame-of-reference, with the viewpoint character generally front and center, constantly in the thick of things so the "I" character gets a reader very personally involved with the action as the story unfolds.

Writing from the first-person point-of-view has some advantages. It usually results in very strong reader identification, creates intensity of emotion, and causes good pacing and tension.

By the same token there are some drawbacks to using the first-person point-of-view, as it does have its limitations. The viewpoint character can't know certain things if she wasn't at the scene, so other techniques must be used to impart that information—such as overhearing a conversation, being told something by a third party, through the use of speculation, etcetera.

Using the "I" viewpoint creates a sense of intimacy on the page and it can do a lot to convey the mood of a narrator, or create an atmosphere for the locale as in my story, "I Auctioned My Body to the Highest Bidder!" published by *Exciting Confessions*.

> All evening long snow had been falling. The temperature was just below freezing and snow came down in big, gentle flakes with no wind to whip them into deep drifts. Instead they created a soft blanket of snow on the frozen ground.
>
> I had been sitting at my upstairs window, looking down on the street, when I heard the whoosh of air brakes and turned to see one of the McKnelly Trucking Line rigs pull up our street, round the corner, and swing off the boulevard and proceed to the warehouses behind their property.
>
> Within ten minutes another eighteen-wheeler rounded the corner, then flipped the amber clearance lights on and off. When the driver got right in front of our house, he hauled on the lumbering Peterbilt's air horn, and the moaning blast caused sympathy vibrations that almost rattled the windows out of our house.
>
> I knew then that Chuck McKnelly, my boyfriend, was in off the road and my heart skipped a beat when I realized that in a matter of a few minutes I'd see him again.

First-person techniques allow a writer to impart a vast amount of information in a brief scene, and make the action come to life by appealing to the five senses.

7.2 Overcoming Self-Consciousness in First-Person Viewpoint

The biggest problem most aspiring authors seem to have with writing in the first-person viewpoint—particularly in the confession field—are their initial feelings of embarrassment. Sometimes inexperienced writers have a bit of difficulty because they are not able to easily dissociate the "I-character" from the "I-self" and their inhibitions cause them some problems, because subconsciously they fear that readers will attribute the actions and choices of the "I-character" to the "I-self" behind the keyboard and think poorly of them. A bit of practice and working with very diverse "I-characters" usually rectifies this psychological aspect of writing in first-person viewpoint.

Writing from the first-person viewpoint is not difficult. It should come to you as easily as talking about yourself to a friend using the same intimate, conversational, colloquial style you'd use to describe a situation if you were chatting over a cup of coffee across your kitchen table.

7.3   Who Tells the Story—The Woman or the Man?

When you set out to write a confession story, one viewpoint option where you'll have a choice is whether you'll craft a story from a female or male viewpoint.

Since the majority of confessions have female narrators (if only because the audience is primarily comprised of women of varying ages), reading several published stories should give you a "feel" for the feminine viewpoint if you are not female. And if you are, simply write what comes naturally.

A few men do read confession magazines regularly but the editors tend not to cater to them. They will, however, include an occasional male viewpoint story if it's well done, realistic, believable, and focuses on a situation women readers can relate to.

If the confession story is from the male point of view, this should be apparent at the outset so the reader will not assume that the narrator is female, and then a bit later be rudely jarred from the smooth flow of the story by discovering that "I" is not a woman.

Specifying the narrator's gender can be done easily and unobtrusively, by having the male narrator identified by name as close to the opening sentence as possible.

> I parked the car at Baylor Lake, and reached for my girlfriend, Janie.
>
> "Gary, no. . . ." she murmured, sighing, almost impatiently, as she pulled away from me. She clenched her hands in her lap. Then, suddenly she began to pick frenziedly at my heavy ID bracelet I'd placed on her wrist six months before. "I—I feel awful, Gary," she went on in a tear-filled, squeaky voice. "But—but I've found someone else. A guy I met at camp this summer. Take your bracelet back. I don't want it any more."
>
> I held out my hand. She dropped the chain link bracelet into my cupped palm. The precious metal was warm from her skin. I stared at it, unable to speak.
>
> Apparently, neither could she.
>
> "Well," I finally managed, and my voice came out a whistle. "I guess there's not much to say, huh?"

"Nothing, except . . . Gary, I'm really sorry."

"Me, too. It was fun while it lasted," I said, hating my tight tone as I tried to sound casual. I reached for the key in the ignition.

"I'll always think you're the greatest, Janie."

She gave me a wan smile. "Same here," she said.

Things were stiff on the way back to town. We were both trying too hard to be civilized and to act like everything was all right, when as far as I was concerned, things couldn't have been more wrong.

When Janie slammed the car door behind her, it was like something deep inside me died, and I knew it was really over.

Any confession narrator who decides to write in the male point-of-view works in the field with a distinct handicap, since over 90 percent of the published confession stories will tell the woman's side of things. That means that the writer's male-viewpoint stories must be truly exceptional to win a slot in a magazine's monthly makeup. Those who really want to write in the male point-of-view might consider submitting to some of the various men's magazines that use "true confession" stories, as chances for success improve at magazines aimed at male readership.

When it comes to writing the male viewpoint story for the female-oriented confession magazines, some writers will try, a few talented story tellers will succeed, but for most writers—who happen to be women—setting out to beat such odds may not be worth the effort required when writing a riveting tale telling the woman's side of the story can be almost guaranteed to meet with success.

"This is too farfetched for me. Where's your motivation?"

"An amusing story, but it's one our readers would never believe because it lacks the right motivation to make it work."

"This is well-written, but not believable. The narrator had no reason to follow through as she did. It didn't make sense and actually led nowhere."

7.4   The Importance of Motivation—Know It and Show It

The difference between a rejected and accepted manuscript is often a matter of motivation. Motivation is one aspect of a story's creation that too often is ignored by novice authors. They have to have a character do something to make the story work, but they don't give the person a strong reason to behave in that particular way, so it has an illogical, phony tone.

When people in real life react to pressures by behaving in strange ways, we shrug it off and accept their quirks. This is not allowed for story people. You can't have them doing something that they ordinarily wouldn't do unless you offer a sound, logical reason to explain such behavior. A confession narrator can't do something on impulse, simply because she felt like it, or doesn't know why she did it. You, the author, must know why—and then show why—so that the motivation is clear.

As the creator of your story, you probably know your characters' motivations. The reader does not. So you must not forget to share this explanatory knowledge via dialogue, narration, or introspection.

The motivation for a character may originate in a desire for revenge, to save face, to protect herself or a loved one from a hurtful truth, etcetera. Real life is full of motivations. Study the people around you, figure out why they've done what they have. Realize that motivation is part of the cause-and-effect scheme of things, and two people in conflict with each other can also present a basis for believable, unusual motivations, as was the case in my story, "I'm Having a Phantom Baby!"

The heroine, who deeply loves a fellow named Tony, is shocked when he insists that she become pregnant before he will consider marrying her. This is certainly not the attitude of the average young man who enjoys his freedom. But then, Tony's background included a brief and bitter marriage that ended in divorce when his wife, after tricking him into marriage, refused to have the children he wanted. This colors his thinking and also provides motivation.

"The next time I get married, it's going to be on my terms," Tony said firmly. Then he took me into his arms and kissed me brutally, his lips almost hurting mine. "I want kids," he murmured, "And I don't intend to beg and plead with my wife to give them to me. I'll marry you, sweetheart, when I have to. Now you know my . . . terms."

My blood raced through my veins as I took the wallet from Tony's hand.

"Don't use one tonight," I whispered bravely. I drew him into my arms, kissing him as he pressed close. "Make me pregnant."

Later on, right before Tony is due to ship out with a fresh Navy assignment, the narrator believes she's pregnant, she entertains the symptoms, she marries Tony, and then is devastated when her physician on base at his new assignment tells her that there is no baby, that she's suffering a false pregnancy, a malady that can occur when a woman very much wants to conceive and for some reason is unable to.

Tony's edict had given her the motivation she needed to desire a baby to the point where her mind tricked her body into experiencing a fake pregnancy, medically known as pseudocyesis.

Motivation can help make a story convincing but you can't count on coincidence or luck to carry the rest of the load, even if truth is stranger than fiction, as the old saying goes.

7.5 Foreshadowing for Believability

Therefore, to make unlikely events you'll need within a story seem not only logical, but plausible, you must pave the way for their appearance through the skillful use of writing tricks known as "plants," a term that refers to foreshadowing.

Plants are hints or clues that are so casually placed within a story that the reader is all but unaware of them, and their significance doesn't become obvious until much later when the story's successful outcome hinges on that little buried fact.

In "I Hired A Man to Love Me," the story about the wife of the male prostitute, it seemed rather incredible that a wife wouldn't know her husband's exact line of work. To explain away the narrator's acceptance I have her aware, in a vague way, that he's a salesman. And, as she explains to her friend, she doesn't have a "good head for business" so she doesn't discuss her husband's new job with him. What matters to her is that he's able to earn a living again, even though it's not the best position in the world and it seems to be taking a lot out of him. Because of this scene, the reader is led astray the same as the wife, and will be just as startled when the husband bursts through the open hotel room door.

In another story, "I Begged My Man to Love Me," published by *Intimate Story*, the man's lack of attempts at hanky-panky begin to really bother the affectionate girlfriend. She sets out to seduce him, and the attempt is a dismal failure. They're both hurt and mortified. He because of his failure, she because she believes she isn't appealing to him, until they face each other, communicate, and the man who loves her admits that he has been left impotent due to sugar diabetes.

That knowledge may come as a surprise to the reader—and the heroine—but in all fairness only because they failed to pick up on the hint tossed out when the narrator served her boyfriend coffee:

> I set the tray on the table and put the coffee pot on a trivet. I offered Curt the sugar and cream but he waved them away.
>
> "Thanks, but I take mine black. No sugar. Doctor's orders," he explained. "Nice kids you have," he changed the subject. "How long were you married?"

Foreshadowing is at its best when plants are slipped in unobtrusively so that the reader is not aware of them until the story's climax when a detail becomes necessary for the plot to work, and does so without leaving the reader feeling cheated because important information was purposely withheld. But be aware that if a plant is too obvious it can give your story away prematurely. So always work your plants in as early as possible, as deftly as you can, and know that you've played fair-and-square with your readers to give them the clues they require to understand a satisfying and riveting story.

7.6   Selecting an Appropriate Time Frame

Some stories cover a period of time that's a matter of hours, some span a week or two, most cover several months, and then there are stories that may encompass a period of time amounting to decades.

7.7   Using Transitions

Editors know the work of a beginning writer when they open up a manuscript and are confronted with myriad details of arising from bed, showering, brushing teeth, putting on makeup, dressing, having breakfast, going to the car, driving to work, and arriving at the office because they realize they're seeing the work of an author who doesn't understand how transitions are used to show the passage of time and successfully link the major scenes.

Some possible examples of workable transitions to show the passage of time:

The hands on the clock hanging over the teacher's desk seemed to crawl by. As the instructor droned on, I felt myself getting sleepy, and before I knew it the bell shrilled, signalling the end of the day. It'd take me a half an hour to walk across town. Then I'd know if the job was mine or not.

This reveals the passage of a brief portion of the day.
What about when more time slips by between major scenes?

Hours went by, compiling to become days, then the days added up to become weeks. Finally, the big day arrived.

Or to show that not mere weeks—but months—have gone by between one scene and another.

At the Cape winter howled its last and gave way to the first balm of spring, then spring's cool hush departed to make way for summer's heat and the milling, sunburned crowds. I knew soon that I'd see Andy again. . . .

Years?

My heart stood still when I saw him. For a stunning moment it was as if I'd been spun back in time, for although ten years had passed, to me he looked exactly as he had when we'd been forced to part.

Transitions need not be flowery or poetic, although those kinds can be very effective. Simplicity works, too:

Twenty-four hours later. . . .
    By nightfall. . . .
    Almost before it seemed possible. . . .

Transitions are meant to cover a period of general inaction within a story as quickly as possible, therefore, do not "take your time" making the move from one major scene to another!

7.8   Writing to Be Readable

Purple prose, or overwriting, is one of the most glaring faults of the beginning confession writer. When new authors are unsure of how to realistically convey deep emotion, they often attempt to do it by using grandiose adjectives. As a result the story narrative sounds artificial and editors will rarely purchase such stylistically flawed efforts even if the plot is good.

Some editors refer to the "Lowest Common Denominator Reader," as the prototype reader that an author should keep in mind when preparing a manuscript. Confession readers run the gamut as there are some highly educated people in the audience, and some who have not received sufficient schooling to have earned certificates attesting to a formal education.

Therefore, editors want authors to keep the overall audience in mind and write a story that the well-educated person can enjoy, but to do it in a way so that the person who hasn't had a lot of formal education can understand and enjoy the piece, too.

In the confession field, if you have a character "grimace," the editor may change it to "frown," which is a simpler word. Don't have characters "imbibe" when everyone knows that people take a drink. Don't have characters have a "repast" when almost any reader would readily understand "snack." And a man who is "drunk" will be understood by all readers, even those who might not get the drift if he is described as "inebriated." All readers can envision a "toothless old man," but few will successfully envision the fellow if he's described as "an endentulous octogenarian."

7.9   How to Be a Sensual Writer

When drafting the manuscript, strive to make it a sensual experience for the reader by providing details that appeal to the reader's personal memory bank of vivid experiences compiled during a lifetime of living.

Most persons have within their minds a great storehouse of specific memories such as the creamy feel of chocolate fudge melting upon the tongue, the sharp tang of ammonia, acrid stench of burning hair, the odor of a wet dog, the texture of silk, the blat of a civil defense air raid siren, or the feathery purple clouds and glowing sky of a flaming pink sunset over the Pacific Ocean.

So with these sensory perceptions "on file," the reader can instantly recall the experience whenever the reader sees a word or phrase in print that jogs the memory. Writing that is crafted to focus on appealing to the five senses—*sound, touch, sight, hearing, smell*—makes the reader feel that she's really lived through the experience while reading because the sensory stimulation was so acute.

Such is the case when Bubbles, Aggie-Anne Carson in "Men Won't Marry a Tramp Like Me," is witnessing some rodeo action:

> When the rodeo announcer's voice echoed over the public address system, the crowd roared. (Sound) I ran to the wooden fence and clawed my way up the rough, splintered planks. (Touch) A Brahman bull thrashed in the chute before he bucked into the arena. The huge beast twisted and spun. Mark's legs flew into the air. A patch of daylight appeared between Mark and the bull. (Sight) My mouth went dry and metallic with fear. (Taste) A powerful hind leg crashed down and landed on Mark's pelvis and slid off. (Sight) Mark screamed in agony (Sound) and clutched himself as he writhed in pain. The bull whirled away, kicking and lurching around the corral (Sight) in a cloud of choking dust mingled with the musky scent of animal sweat. (Smell)

Writing the scene with a lot of sensory detailing is much more effective than if the narrator had explained:

> I climbed the rungs of the corral in time to see Mark thrown off the bull and trampled.

It takes a little conscious effort, and perhaps even a "cheat sheet" listing the five senses tacked up on your bulletin board as a visual aid to remind you what senses to appeal to, but it's certainly an effect worth working to achieve.

7.10 Creating Realistic Dialogue

Confession dialogue is an "edited" version of actual conversation. In real life, people often say the same thing in three ways, thinking that they are making three new points when they are simply repeating one. Repetition in conversation is not easily caught or even noticed by the ear, but in written dialogue the eye will almost always notice it. So if your characters have something to say, let them say it once—and then get on with the next thought. This moves the story ahead and keeps the dialogue brisk and lively.

In narrative, it may take pages to delineate clearly what the narrator and other characters are like. Dialogue, on the other hand, can frequently accomplish this same task in a very concise manner:

> "What do you say we go out on Saturday night?" Jake drawled. He smiled down at me and his eyes swept over me like an intimate caress. I swallowed hard. Butterflies batted around in my stomach.
>
> "I—I don't know," I stammered. A hot flush spread over my cheeks as his undivided attention was focused on me.
>
> Jake chuckled. "Sure you do," he said, in a tone that was so self-assured. He smoothed a stray wisp of hair away from my crimson cheeks. "You want to go out with me as much as I want you to. Admit it!"

Jake sounds cocky and sure of himself. The narrator? Shy and inexperienced.

In real life good conversational manners are often ignored. People interrupt one another all the time. Confession characters do it, too—and it quickens the tempo of the story as in the following:

> "Sure I love you, sweetheart," Royce said in a smooth tone as he turned away from me and dried his face with a fluffy white towel. "Whatever made you think that I didn't?"
>
> "Because of the way you act!" I broke in. My voice shook with anger and nervousness. "You—you used to be so thoughtful, gentle, and caring. You acted like I was the only girl in the world. You never took me for granted. Now it's like—it's like—"
>
> "Like what?" Royce prompted innocently as he leaned close to the mirror to examine his freshly shaved chin. As he reached for his cologne his eyes flicked up to meet mine in the steamy bathroom mirror. I tore my gaze away from his taunting glance.
>
> "Like a swinging single," I spat the words. "You're always . . . on the make!"

7.11 Punctuation to Give Dialogue Power

Dashes are useful in writing dialogue. They give the effect of urgency. A few stuttered words can lend credibility to a nervous, upset, or deceitful character. The elliptical, broken, or unfinished sentence, indicated by dots . . . is a good way to make dialogue read with the rhythm of a spoken sentence, and it allows the author to capture the special cadence needed to express "pregnant pauses," telling silences, and other conversational overtones that make no sound but can work visually on the printed page.

Beware of overusing exclamation points. Selected as needed they can give realism to dialogue, but . . . overused they're like too much garlic!

And occasionally, although rarely, nothing works quite so well to signal exactly how a remark was made, as the question mark coupled with an exclamation point.

"*You what?*" seems vapid compared to the visibly shocked: "*You what?!*"

These various technical tricks, from expert foreshadowing, to succinct transitions, to sensual writing, to carefully crafted dialogue, with everything underscored by logical, believable, visible motivation, can be perfected as you revise your manuscript once you've finished your first draft.

The beginning confession writer will probably need two to three additional drafts to polish the manuscript for submission. But don't despair, simply remind yourself of what selling professionals already know: *Rewriting is the key to salable writing.*

Section II

WRITING
THE
FACTUAL
PERSONAL
EXPERIENCE
ARTICLE

Introduction to Section II

Factual personal experience stories are "true"—they really happened—but that does not necessarily mean that editors expect "the truth, the whole truth, and nothing but the truth." Most of them do allow—and at times even suggest—the literary license necessary to tailor an author's effort to exactly fit their publication's particular slant.

In writing the fictional confession story, we were concerned with setting, character, viewpoint, theme, etcetera, as they had bearing on how we plotted the story, with these combined elements guiding us as we sought to select the most satisfying plot sequence from the various possibilities.

In a slightly different manner, in writing the true experience story we will still be concerned with these concepts—setting, character, viewpoint, and plot—although we'll be working within the parameters of reality instead of exploring the boundaries of imagination, and will be adhering to the journalistic focus of: *who, what, when, where, how*, and *why*, sometimes answering all these questions, other times addressing only a few.

In the factual true experience story, human behavior in the form of action and reaction on the part of the given real-life characters, has already dictated story line elements and has isolated the basic conflict, or unusual situation or phenomenon. The factual personal experience article has a specific beginning, middle, and end based upon concrete facts. Therefore, in writing the true experience story, there's not a lot of mental mulling over required, as you're provided a set group of components to work with as soon as you discern that a situation you've either experienced personally or been told about by another individual could be rendered into a marketable manuscript.

In the strictest technical terms, however, you must still "plot" the story, in that you have to be selective and consciously decide which facts to include, which to omit, decide in what order you will present the story line, and from whose point-of-view (first-person, third-person, or as-told-to) so that the organization and presentation of the facts creates a manuscript as entertaining and riveting as its fictional counterpart.

The factual article, too, ideally should have some form of take-away value to leave with the reader, be it merely an unusual phenomenon to ponder and puzzle over with friends, a religious philosophy to consider, basic how-to skills smoothly inserted into a personal experience wildlife article, or merely providing a hearty laugh as the reader relates to a humor article centering on an experience common to the human condition.

As you think back over your existence and recall things that have happened to you that provided valuable lessons in dealing with problems, you may be delighted to discover that you'll be able to draw upon your own circumstances and turn them into personal experience stories written from the "I" point-of-view, with you able to either take full credit with your legal name, or shield your identity with a pen name.

Or perhaps you may have heard of an interesting event and realize it has the makings of a good story if you can interview those involved, hone in on their feelings, insights, actions, and capture the sense of time and place and the dramatic urgency so that you're able to write an "I" viewpoint story from their point-of-view, but with you as the author in an "as-told-to" story.

Or perhaps the situation dictates that you render the manuscript from the third person point-of-view, with you as the bylined author, but with the lead character, the subject about whom you are writing, referred to by a given name and applicable pronouns, with the writing technique the same as for a third person point-of-view fictional story.

In the writing of factual personal experiences pieces you can either use real identities, or you can provide aliases to protect innocent people (or yourself), so that those who've served as the basis for the story will not recognize themselves.

This is an especially valuable option if it's your personal experience and you want to tell *your story* and do not wish to concern yourself with getting another's permission to do so, particularly if the person integral to your true-life story has proven antagonistic.

In this event, it's also a good idea to publish the manuscript under a pen name—something most editors readily agree to—if there's a sensitive aspect to the piece that could prove angering or embarrassing to those with whom the author interacted. It's always wise to err on the side of caution.

If you wish to build a lucrative career writing true-life stories, it's a good idea to start drawing up a list of possible articles you can write. Your personal accounts are the most logical place to begin as you work to get a feel for the format. Rendering your own experiences into manuscripts will give you the credibility that editors look for when acquiring manuscripts. Plus, *you were there*, so you'll be able to accurately convey a sense of mood, atmosphere, drama, and sensual stimuli so that the reader can vicariously "live" your experience as he or she reads the article. And the writing should be as easy as telling the story to a friend over coffee.

Once you have jotted some notes in a journal or logbook that can serve as a repository for ideas, it's time to consult the marketing books to assess the salability of your planned properties.

The annual *Writer's Market*, published by Writer's Digest Books, is an excellent reference manual to consult. The various categories have markets neatly grouped, allowing you to see what magazines are interested in publishing the kinds of manuscripts you have in mind, where they are located, how frequently they are published, circulation, pay rates, and other helpful information to help you make comparisons.

This search process serves as an indicator to help you decide if it's worth your time to work on a specific idea, for you'll be able to discern at the outset if chances for eventually selling the manuscript are solid even if you happen to strike out with the first publication you submit to.

Generally the various individual category listings in the *Writer's Market* will range from large publications with national or international distribution, on down to tiny uncopyrighted periodicals that command the attention of only a small region of the country. Pay rates are usually equally as diverse although their basic subject interests are almost exactly the same whether the publication is a major or minor player in the category.

It's not uncommon for new authors to tend to undersell their talents, so as you market your manuscripts keep in mind that it's a fiscally sound idea to go for the top-paying markets, first and foremost, because we are in this business to make money. You can always work your way down to the lesser-paying markets. Only after exhausting those that issue checks should you consider submitting to the "pays in copies" publications.

There are times when an author, who is a newcomer to the industry, may consider it a fair tradeoff to be paid in copies or with a subscription if it means breaking into print and establishing some *bona fide* publishing credits. But only you can know when you've reached the point where "payment in copies" is justified—as it can be—if it means the difference between placing a piece or having it remain unpublished in your desk drawer.

In the fictional confession field, it's standard that publishers will want to acquire all rights so that the author has no further claim to the work whatsoever. In the factual personal experience industry, there is great leeway in what rights publishers seek to gain, and there's a lot more negotiating room, so a good strategy is to *always* keep as many rights as you are able.

Generally I've found publishers to be very agreeable in allowing me to retain rights so that I am free to resell the same manuscript time and again as I seek out markets with the same basic interest, but whose audiences or geographical areas do not overlap. Because I resisted selling All Rights, and was prepared to intelligently argue my point if an editor contacted me to offer an acceptance, I almost always won the desired concessions from the publishers involved.

While sometimes the checks, per sale, may seem modest, and you may occasionally have to settle for a slightly reduced fee to keep some rights, it's usually a good career move. That way it doesn't take long to build a valuable inventory of manuscripts you can offer for one-time reprint rights for years and years to come. The individual checks may be small, but the combined payment can add up to a very impressive sum.

Each form of personal experience writing has its own special aspects that set it apart from the true-life stories published by totally unrelated magazines. But if you keep in mind the fiction writing techniques that can make any personal experience come alive, and give the reader the "you are there" feeling, you can likely find success in almost any area of true-life story writing that you should choose to explore.

CHAPTER
8

Writing for the General and Religious Women's Magazines

Writing the true-life story for the women's magazines, whether the publication is secular or religious, much parallels crafting the fictional "confession" story. The format is almost exactly the same. Sometimes the only difference is that one story is fiction, the other true.

8.1 Finding Suitable Ideas

The range of acceptable topics and subjects is probably as broad as the range of human experience. Some problems that have been used are: being a compulsive gambler, getting arrested for shoplifting, becoming addicted to prescription drugs, marrying a homosexual, overcoming an eating disorder, dealing with rape, coping with being a compulsive spender.

The list goes on and on.

A look through women's magazines gives a view into what topics are timely.

"Back From The Brink" in *Marriage Partnership*, a religious publication, deals with the no-holds-barred true-life story of a couple's struggle to save their floundering marriage.

"Killer or Victim?," in *Ladies' Home Journal*, focused on the story of a battered woman who struck back and spent time in jail for killing her husband until a governor's pardon freed her.

"The Street Kid and the Reporter," the true-life "A Mother's Story" column in *Redbook Magazine*, was by a journalist on assignment to cover homeless children, a professional who wasn't supposed to get involved but then met a young boy who, "Once I told his story, he rewrote mine."

Today's Christian Woman also printed a piece about homelessness, "A Friend in Need," with the narrator a person who never thought that her friend could end up among the homeless.

"Why I Date Your Husband," a true-life confession, in *Redbook*, was by a woman who explained her preference for married men as a warning for wives to heed.

"I Was Sterilized," was the true account of a young single woman who explained her decision to *Cosmopolitan*'s audience.

"I Gave Up My Children," published by *Ladies' Home Journal*, was the riveting story of a woman who gave away her children from an unhappy first marriage when she and her husband were too immature to be good parents and offer her children what she wanted them to have.

"Secrets of an Exercise Dropout-Turned-Zealot," in *SELF*, is the story of a woman a lot of us can relate to, who got with a physical fitness program that she's managed to stay with, as she says, "So far."

Today's Christian Woman published "The Most Terrifying Night of My Life," the true-life story told by a rape victim.

Quite another personal experience was the basis for the article "I Married the Man Who Raped Me," featured in *Woman's World*.

"Granny's Plant Lesson," in *Confident Living*, is the poignant story of how a grandmother's wisdom offers the solution for a descendant to save her marriage.

"City Mouse, Country Mouse," in *Redbook* dealt with a simple, true-life story, that of a young woman from the city who marries a fellow from the country, and she details how their marriage became rocky because of city-country conflicts, but then shares the successful solution she found that led to a harmonious union.

And another *Woman's World* true-life story, "I Sold Myself to Pay My Son's Medical Bills," shares a desperate experience with a sympathetic audience.

Also in *Woman's World* was "It's Hard Letting Go Of Your Daughter," a father's story, written about his ordeal when his thirteen-year-old girl fell in love with an eighteen-year-old boy, and she's set on marrying him, and does, with her father's blessing.

If you have a problem, and if you can focus on it, tell it in riveting terms using fiction techniques to make the article come alive for the reader. If you can make it as diverse as the women's magazines using this type material, it's almost certain that you can eventually find a home for your personal experience manuscript.

8.2   A Subtle Difference—Religious vs. Secular

About the only difference between a manuscript suitable to submit to the secular market and one for the religious field is that in the religious magazines, there's a focus on God.

This is not a heavy-handed treatment but simply a quiet statement of faith. When all else failed, usually the narrator, at her wits' end, has nowhere else to turn but to the Creator. And in that action discovered the wisdom, strength, or change in attitude required to solve even the worst problems.

In the secular story, however, often that insight will come from another person, instead of through Scripture. The healing of an attitude or problem situation may be the result of social institutions—recovery groups, a good therapist, a self-help book, a friend's advice, etcetera.

8.3   Getting Personal About Writing Personal
Experience Articles

You need not write about scandalous or earth-shaking, headline-grabbing true experiences although chances of finding easy acceptance are probably greater for such an article.

But if in the course of living you've made some mistakes you've later regretted and have learned from, those experiences—everyday problems others probably also face—are the raw material for acceptable manuscripts if you write them in a factual manner, blend in believability, sincerity, and offer emotional impact and helpful solutions.

The true-life stories arising from your own existence, especially those that make you "squirm" as you recall them, are usually the ideas that are most salable. In the event that you want to tell your story honestly and intimately, but without being embarrassed by being publicly identified with the problem situation, it is advisable—and acceptable—to use a pen name to protect your privacy. But you should make this clear at the outset when you submit to an editor, or simply send it in under your chosen pen name. Also, alert your letter carrier that you may have manuscripts returning under a pen name. Then if you have work accepted, simply bank the acceptance check as you would a two-party check, and declare the earnings on your tax return.

8.4   How to Structure the Religious Personal Experience Article

In the nonfiction true-life article, as with the fictional confession story, it is necessary to identify the conflict as close to the opening paragraphs as possible, as I did in my story, "The True Gift of Christmas," a seasonal piece published in *Faith at Work, Nazarene Standard,* and later in *Unity Magazine.*

> " 'Tis the season to be jolly. . . ."
> The carol playing on the radio mocked me. I was anything but jolly.
> For me the season had been a series of disappointments: frightening medical problems, setbacks in the construction of our new home, and the sad news that my parents would be unable to come for our long-planned Christmas visit due to my father's emergency surgery.
> As Christmas neared the hardwood trees outside were stark, and the ground was barren and covered with matted brown grass. Instead of fluffy, white snow there were only clods of frozen mud. It definitely wasn't Christmas outside.
> Even though the bushy pine tree was decorated, packages in pretty paper were nestled under its sweeping boughs, and the usual candles and Yuletide arrangements were in place, with greeting cards arriving in every mail delivery, it wasn't Christmas inside either.
> "Perhaps it will really seem like Christmas to me when I'm in church on Christmas Eve," I said to a friend. "If I don't get the Christmas spirit then—I never will."

The mood for the story is created, and the problem—not feeling the Christmas spirit—is one that many people can relate to because they've experienced it on a personal level.

So it was time to introduce the conflict and make things go "from bad to worse."

Two nights before Christmas, my husband came home with news: "Joe and Jean (not their real names) are coming over on Christmas Eve."

For a moment I wasn't sure I'd heard him right. I stared at Steve as awful memories flooded over me. I recalled the painful, unpleasant scene almost exactly three years before when our friendship had dissolved and I felt as if I'd taken back my life and that of my family, from another's possession.

In narration, I share with the reader what was going through my mind. In this brief scene the audience becomes privy to why I'm less than thrilled with the idea of entertaining this couple. Childless, they'd doted on my children, spoiled them outrageously, contrived with my kids to keep secrets from Mommy, undermined my discipline, and I suffered in silence, my misery festering, until one day— enough was enough!—and I exploded and severed all ties.

The past three years had been the most peaceful of my life. I couldn't believe that my husband had issued an invitation that could open up a Pandora's box of problems.

"How on earth did that happen?" I asked.

Steve glanced at me. "I invited them," he admitted, almost defiantly.

"You what?!" I asked. "Why on earth did you do something like that?"

He didn't answer.

Tears salted my voice. "Christmas is supposed to be spent with your family and loved ones," I raged. I felt suddenly weak all over and my voice grew thin and reedy. "Not . . . not with . . ."

My words cracked off. I couldn't quite push out the truth: enemies!

"They were going to be all alone," Steve murmured.

Silence mushroomed between us.

"Are they coming for supper?" I muttered.

"I didn't invite them to eat with us. But you can, if you want to. . . ."

The problem has been identified, the conflict has been intensified, a resolution must be sought, which, initially I did by hoping that if I did nothing the situation would fix itself.

Perhaps Joe and Jean sensed when Steve had invited them that it was by his invitation and not shared by me. Perhaps they wouldn't even show up, I thought, and the idea gave me hope.

But when I visualized the couple in their sixties, childless, no close family, all alone in the world, I couldn't help but feel ashamed of myself.

A little more narrative introspection, and I, just as would a fictional confession heroine, reached my "moment of truth."

I looked back over the past three years, and I saw clearly the changes that had occurred within me. I had grown and become stronger in my own identity. So had my children, now in school, and old enough to be reasoned with and to differentiate between gifts and the value of parental love. I also no longer hid my feelings, stewing in silence, letting others walk all over me while I said nothing in hopes that the unpleasantness would pass before I reached the snapping point. Surely as I had changed, so had Joe and Jean.

At this "climax" of the true-life story, I picked up the telephone, and checked the phone book for a number that I'd once memorized, and I sounded warm and welcoming as I invited them to come early and share a Christmas meal with us.

And I quickly moved on to the happy ending:

. . . The three cold years melted away in the warmth of renewed friendships. Bad times went unmentioned. We found ourselves visiting non-stop, catching up on the events that had taken place in the years that had elapsed. The evening flew by and midnight came. Christmas arrived before our guests departed.

And at this point, the thematic, take-away message is summarized for the readers' benefit and to neatly complete the episode:

The godly gifts I received that night from our special guests far outshone the material things for me wrapped under the Christmas tree, as I got the true spirit and meaning of Christmas in my life, and from Joe and Jean received a 'Christmas to Remember'. . . .

8.5 More on How to Structure a Religious
Personal Experience Article

Christian Home & School magazine published another article based on a serious problem that a lot of young mothers can relate to, and I bared my heart in "The Peaceable Kingdom," hoping that others could find help in my personal solutions.

> I fought back tears as I chopped the cabbage into slaw. Mom went by and touched my shoulder comfortingly. Through the window I saw the car carrying my husband, father, and two children disappear down the lane heading toward town.
>
> I gave a helpless sniffle and pinched my eyes tight.
>
> Mom cleared her throat. "Kids didn't used to be this way," she said.
>
> As a school teacher, recently a finalist for "Minnesota State Teacher of the Year," I realized that she knew what she was talking about. But I was past the point of being comforted by the assurance that dozens of parents my mother knew were suffering similarly.
>
> "I don't envy parents having to rear children in this day and age. It's tough enough being a parent without your kids being affected by the bad things they see on television, or the conduct of children whose parents don't care what they do."
>
> I nodded, too choked up to talk. I was still smarting from the argument with my defiant nine-year-old daughter, Marie, that had finally evolved into heated words with my husband.
>
> At that point Dad had suggested that they all go to the mall. Their departure left the house pleasantly devoid of children.

The setting has been sketched in, the atmosphere made clear to the reader, and the problem—sassy, argumentative children—leads to the additional conflict of the basic problem causing difficulties in the marriage relationship.

Narrative introspection briefly acquaints the reader with how the situation had evolved from minor episodes of unacceptable behavior when the children were small, to almost constant difficulties.

> For the past several years our family life had gone down hill by degrees. My husband and I loved each other deeply, but with the turmoil and tension, our relationship sometimes seemed to erode

bit by bit, day in, day out, as we fought over the children's behavior.

The problems all started when our son and daughter began to attend school. Their infrequent sassy remarks began recurring with regularity. Overnight they seemed convinced that they knew all that there was to know. Soon the sassing turned to outright disobedience. Shortly, sibling rivalry reared its ugly head; close behind came the get-even tattling tactics.

I hoped it was "just a stage" and one day I would wake up and they'd have grown beyond it. Instead, I arose each morning, hating to face the day, knowing it would be a carbon copy of the day before: a day filled with rancor, disobedience, sassing.

I knew that such negative feelings couldn't be normal or healthy. Something had to be done.

As with the fictional confession story heroine, I sought to find workable solutions only to meet with failure as the conflicts intensified.

Spock was outdated, so I turned to Ginott. He sounded good in theory, but when I tried to apply it, I failed miserably. I discovered that I couldn't "dialogue constructively" all by myself and my children wanted no part of these "talks."

Then I tried the "good, old-fashioned spanking," which old timers vowed would cure disobedience, smart mouths, and quarrelsomeness. But it, too, had drawbacks. I felt guilty. And I worried about crossing the fine line between discipline and abuse.

Bit by bit, I abandoned the experts and slipped back into the reflex action of all young mothers I knew, and a prime source of irritation to all of their husbands: yelling, threatening, and being caught up in pointless, heated arguments with children.

As in the fictional confession story, after a heroine has muddled along with the situation going from bad to worse, an individual far enough removed from the conflict to view it objectively offers insights that put the problem into perspective, so that the narrator is able to see things from a fresh frame-of-reference and rethink attitudes and behavior and arrive at a more positive solution.

Such is almost always the case in the true-life articles in women's magazines. Sometimes outside input works and the article quickly ends on an upbeat note. Other times, that option too, fails, as it did for me in "The Peaceable Kingdom," and I was forced to look further for an answer to a very serious problem.

> With disturbing frequency, I lost my temper and fled the scene in tears, proclaiming the children victorious if only by default. My tears were tears of anger, failure, frustration and self-loathing. I was losing control of my life. And I had begun to hate the woman my children had turned me into.
>
> "Marie seems to really enjoy goading you," Mom said, interrupting my thoughts as I stirred the cabbage salad.
>
> "I know. . . ." I'd suspected that for a long time, and it was small comfort to know that it was evident to observers.
>
> "She just pulled a neat trick on you and Steve. She divided-and-conquered like a pro."
>
> Until that moment I hadn't even realized that. My thoughts flew back to the many times when I'd reached a decision, and minutes later she was pestering her dad, wanting my decision reversed. Many times she succeeded, but only because he was unaware I'd already given an answer.
>
> "Why don't you try a trick I use in the classroom?" Mom suggested. "The next time Marie tries to get you involved in a pointless argument, tell her you're busy, but that you'll be glad to consider her views if she'll put them in writing." Mom smiled. "If nothing else—it'll result in good penmanship. And if she has to put out some effort to argue with you, she may soon decide that it's not worth the trouble and she'll give up."

I'd tried everything else. So why not? What perhaps worked in the classroom, however, I found failed within the home.

> I had tried everything—everything but God—and there was only one direction for me to take. I was numb as I retrieved the Bible from the bookshelf. The children stared at me as I sat down to read. Minutes later they began to quarrel and jostle. Quietly I asked them to be a little less rambunctious so that I could concentrate. To my surprise—they obeyed.

Reading Scripture, a new experience for me, left me finding it easier to cope, especially when I discovered references to child-rearing in the Old and New Testaments, so I realized problem children were not my problem alone.

I found a change coming over our household. I flew off the handle less. I was regaining my self-respect. Love and admiration was evident in my husband's eyes. And he was backing me 100 percent. He knew I was trying. Really trying. Wanting to preserve the new serenity within the home. When Steve recognized that the children were feeling their oats and wanted to goad me into an interesting encounter, a sharp, "That's enough!" from him settled the matter.

The article offered a happy ending, and then a departing philosophy that readers could accept as a take-away message.

> Our home became a pleasant place to live, and our family became closer and more united and loving. Just as I had to show my children how to tie their shoelaces many, many times before they learned for themselves, so children live what they learn and by correcting my attitudes, I changed theirs. I no longer yelled at them with suggestions for their improved behavior—I showed them how to live. . . .

While both of these true-life stories were published in religious magazines for women, which is a wide-open market with many publications, either problem could've been slanted as successfully toward the "slick" women's publications and a different solution had one of the earlier attempts worked.

Nowadays people are very open about admitting to weakness, seeking help, and there are various recovery groups to help a person find relief from almost any serious problem. This attitude is reflected in the major women's magazines for both secular and religious audiences, and if correctly handled, I doubt that there is any problem too taboo to address. If it's a serious problem afflicting human beings, then it's a situation that editors feel is worth exploring for the readership.

8.6 Structuring the Secular Personal Experience Article

But you don't have to write about deep, dark, secret problems to find success in writing true-life stories for the women's publications. We all like to read heart-warming stories, too, and if you've experienced situations that are especially touching, given the proper treatments, these too can meet with success and inspire readers as you share a poignant episode from your reality.

Such was the case with "A Father's Love," a secular seasonal story, arising from our family's life.

Flies buzzed in the August heat. Sweat trickled to burn in our eyes as we made a load of firewood toward the winter's supply needed to heat our home.

"I sure wish I had a horse," my ten-year-old daughter, Marie, said and gave a wistful sigh. "Do you think maybe sometime I can get a horse, Mom?"

I glanced at her father, bent over the log he was splitting with an axe. "Honey, you know how your dad feels about horses," I murmured. Bit on the cheek by a stallion when he was a youngster, my husband's sentiments regarding all horses were well known. Horses and root canals ranked in a class by themselves.

It seemed like the end of the subject. I had no idea that the kids' dad, who, like most men, could be selectively deaf, had overheard the whispered conversation.

The holidays were bearing down fast, and I felt frazzled by Christmas shopping. One night Steve arrived home late. He walked into the house, gestured for me to follow him into the bedroom, shut the door and began to whisper.

"Have you got Marie anything for Christmas?"

"A few things. Why?"

"I bought her a horse."

"You what?!"

"I bought her a horse," he repeated. "She's been a good kid this past year, more obedient, helping around the farm. I figured this'll probably be the last year she believes in Santa Claus. I thought we'd try to give her what she really wants."

"But a horse? You hate horses!"

A deferring shrug served as his response.

The perfect Christmas seemed well underway. But the most carefully laid plans have a way of going awry, and our special Christmas surprise threatened to disintegrate at every turn.

The owner of the horse had received more—and larger—offers than what my husband had paid him. A mutual friend informed us that previously the owner had backed out of deals to sell the little Appaloosa filly. It was suggested that we take possession of the horse—fast! But we had nowhere to keep her—which would allow us to keep the surprise intact.

"Our worries are over. I have the horse. The guy won't back out now."

"Thank goodness. How did you manage it?"

"I didn't do it," Steve admitted.

And the touching truth came out. Steve had tried to get the day off from his job at the post office. Unable to get the time off, one of the city letter carriers, whose day off it was, offered to use his scheduled day off to attend to our interests. He drove to our farm, loaded the heavy steel stock racks onto our truck by himself, and went to collect the horse. Then he delivered her to our neighbor's farm where she'd stay, receiving lots of TLC until "Santa" was scheduled to deliver an eighteen-month-old horse to a little girl.

Christmas Eve day came—and with it—raging flu. Almost everyone in the household was stricken, including our out-of-state visitors.

Steve's fever raged the worst, compounded by an upset stomach, achy joints and chills. Late afternoon came and he sent Mark and Marie skedaddling to finish up their livestock chores. Then he told them to stay in the house and clean their rooms.

Snow was blowing and a raw wind howled over the frozen landscape, ripping around corners, bending trees as gray, snow-laden clouds scudded eastward, racing across the sky.

"Come on," he whispered, giving me a fevered look. "You can drive me over to Olen's."

The roads were patches of glare ice, dark and glassy, between deep drifts, bumper high.

Steve pulled a halter rope from behind the seat of our pickup, he climbed the woven wire fence and hopped into the neighbor's pasture, whistling between his teeth for the horse to come to him. He snapped the lead rope to her halter, then lopped across the steep, snowy hills toward the Salt Creek bottom land so he could skirt the pastures and sneak the horse up through the back forty acres.

For a moment I watched the two proceed across the open crest of the hilltop. The spirited horse flashed her creamy mane and tail and pranced after the tall, sickly man who lunged ahead into the biting wind, staggered through drifts, and hunched into the piercing cold.

I knew that one little girl's heart would burst with joy come Christmas morning . . . and all because of the sacrifices of a man who hated horses.

The horse was safely hidden in the barn. The blizzard worsened, and the temperature plummeted to around twenty-five below zero. Our plans had been to tether the filly to the patio railing, so she'd be visible through the living room window when the kids got up to investigate under the tree. But we weren't about to make a creature leave a snug, warm barn to stand shivering against the elements.

At four in the morning, when Steve had planned to lead the filly down to the yard, instead, he grabbed a piece of paper, pen, and screwed up his brow as he thought, then wrote:

Marie—If you want to hear your Christmas gift nicker, then go out and look beside Dad's corn picker. Love, Santa.

The kids got up, Mark tore into his presents, and although she tried not to look disappointed, Marie had nothing "big" to compare with Mark's presents. I examined the tree and discovered the "note from Santa."

Marie read it, then looked at me. "Mom, what's a 'nicker'?"

I was amazed. I figured that one word would be a dead giveaway. "What do you say we go to the barn and find out?"

"Maybe it's a baby lamb," Mark said as he skipped ahead.

"That'd be fun," Marie replied.

"Marie!" Mark screamed when he entered the barn. "It's not a lamb. IT'S A HORSE!"

A stunned look came to her face and she catapulted ahead and flung her arms, sobbing with joy, around the beautiful Appaloosa's spotted neck.

"Thanks, Mom!" she whispered when Mark was out of earshot. "I know that there's no Santa Claus. Thanks so much!"

At this point, instead of ending the story on a merely happy note, I inserted what was a summation of philosophy to tie together the entire Christmas story so that readers could recognize and remember the legacy of love behind the gift.

> Maybe there's not a man in a red suit, I realized. But Marie saw the spirit of Christmas in the actions of our friends, from the horse-trading buddy to the pal who gave up his day off, to the nearby horse-crazy retired farmer who provided a little girl's horse a temporary home.
>
> The biggest sacrifice came from the man known for hating horses. And try as he does to act like Misty's not special, he doesn't fool us. We know he likes Misty—even if he hates horses. But then there are always exceptions to the rule, especially when sacrificing up an attitude brings great joy to one you love.

8.7   Marketing Your Manuscript to the Women's Magazines

The secular women's magazines tend to pay higher rates for manuscripts, but they also generally wish to acquire all rights. Competition is extremely keen with these big-name major women's magazines, because many readers, who are not professional writers, are inspired to pick up a pen, or peck away at a typewriter, to tell their true-life stories because the magazines, like *Woman's World* run announcements soliciting publishable experiences from readers.

The religious publications don't openly solicit stories from the readership, so competition isn't as stiff. While the religious women's magazines offer smaller acceptance checks, they are flexible to deal with. And as diverse as the market is, it's quite easy—if the author retains rights—to sell the same article many times to magazines that do not overlap. With general inspirational pieces, where the different doctrines do not become an issue, it's possible to resell the exact same true-life story to a variety of denominational publications—Catholic, Lutheran, Methodist, Baptist, non-denominational, etcetera, with no need to rewrite to make it fit the market.

The stories in either general or religious women's magazines do not necessarily have to be based on your own experiences. You can write true accounts from the lives of friends or celebrities, if they are willing to share their stories, and will give you signed permission to do so. In such instances, even though these are not your experiences, you still write them as an emotional first-person point-of-view story. Excellent examples of this type treatment can be found in *Guideposts Magazine,* a non-denominational magazine, that often features the stories of famous people.

These articles are usually presented under a joint byline, such as "Jane Doe with Mary Smith," or "by Jane Doe as told to Mary Smith." But the payment will go to you, the author who does the work on the manuscript for submission.

CHAPTER
9

Writing for the Nature and
Wildlife Magazines

Over the years I have racked up a goodly number of sales to various nature and wildlife-oriented publications. I never connected with the "biggies," but then I never tried them, because in doing my market search before I began to write, I faced the fact at the outset that my personal experience nature and wildlife stories were not in keeping with what some of the huge, slick publications tend to print.

But if you are a serious sportsman, have the outdoor-type experiences that these top-paying, major wildlife markets regularly use (or you know someone who does), and if you tote a professional quality camera as well as a fishing rod or a gun (or have access to another's photographic record of the event), the editors are desirous of considering your submissions.

9.1   Couch Potatoes Welcome to Apply

Oddly enough, I don't even consider myself an outdoors person, so it's a basic fact that I'm not into deep-sea fishing, nor will I ever be. I haven't hunted in Africa's big-game regions, and I don't expect to because I don't want to. I haven't sought to match wits with deer, elk, caribou, moose, or whatever game can be found in the High Country areas of the West. Indeed, I don't even load a shotgun when I have the chance to go in search of the myriad game that can be found on our personal acreage that we've turned into a refuge for wildlife.

Despite my various limitations, I've written a lot of wildlife articles and sold every one, most of them several times over, to a number of similar but non-competitive markets.

I've attained the degree of success I've enjoyed because I've come up with true-life wildlife stories, as I have personally experienced them, and then I sought to write about the events in a friendly, down-home, let's-go-outside-and-have-fun tone.

9.2   Titles and Topics to Trap Editors' Interest

In addition, I always made it a point to focus on topics a bit out of the mainstream, presenting ideas that I was quite certain editors didn't see crossing their desks on a daily basis.

And I always put careful thought into creating catchy titles that I hoped an editor could envision emblazoned as a blurb on the front cover of their magazine the instant my manuscript was removed from the mailing envelope.

Some of the treatments of unorthodox sporting interests, and their titles, that have repeatedly made it into print, are:

Bee Hunting: One Honey of an Idea
Turtle Hunting: Smorgasbord in a Shell
When Froggie Goes Courtin' (He Gets Caught)
"Hogging" Fish Doesn't Mean Being a Glutton
Arrowhead Collecting: Happ(il)y Hunting the Ground
Mushroom Hunting: Very Morel Behavior
Ginseng Hunting: In Search of the Oriental Wonder Plant
Way Down Yonder in the Paw Paw Patch
Persimmon Hunting: Pucker Power Supreme

9.3   Hunting for Markets Where Others Aren't

Most of the publications that I have placed wildlife articles with are midwestern periodicals from as far north as the Canadian border area of Minnesota, down to the Little Egypt region in the "Land Between the Rivers" in Southern Illinois. Publications include such monthly periodicals as *Water, Woods & Wildlife, Illinois Wildlife, MidWest Outdoors, Missouri Conservationist, Wisconsin Sportsman,* etcetera.

These midwestern-based editors, because I was dealing with outdoor topics they knew existed in their areas, knew that their audiences, too, could relate to the articles devoted to what are, admittedly, regional ideas. But I've also had success in selling articles to wildlife magazines as far away as Maryland, when a universal outdoor activity can transcend geographical differences, such as frog-hunting and the lore of hunting dogs.

You needn't be a hunter or fisherman of renown to write for wildlife and nature publications. If there's an unusual outdoor sport, hunting method, or activity in your area, it could be just the ticket to breaking into print.

Keep in mind that not all paying wildlife publications are listed in the market directories so be sure to check the magazine racks in your local store, and pick up sample copies of periodicals that might serve as an outlet for your work so you can study their slant and draw up your own private market listing from information compiled from the masthead page.

Most wildlife publications that are featured in market listings state that they are open to considering personal experience stories, but often in the same sentence they admonish that they do not wish to see the "Me 'n' Joe" story.

The "Me 'n' Joe" treatment is when the author sets out to chronicle a day's hunting trip, and starts writing without having a sharp focus. The writer merely begins at the beginning—with the hunter arising in the wee hours of the morning, while "the wifey" is lying a-bed. After various and sundry delays, they're on their way, arrive at the site and manage to set up camp, burn breakfast, etcetera. The article goes on and on with numerous boring details until finally it ends with the hunter returning home "tired but happy."

Editors don't want true-life stories with this pedestrian-type treatment.

But what they do wish to see are personal experience articles that are concise, sharply focused, and usually are actually a "slice-of-life" episode from an outdoor experience or hunting trip.

9.4   Openers Are Always in Season

Ideally the manuscript should also be tightly written and sufficiently brief to keep the tempo brisk. To develop a good sense of pace in this type article, it's important to get into the story quickly, as I did with "Hogging Fish Doesn't Mean Being a Glutton." In the opening paragraph I sketched in the setting and also captured the mood as I described what is a typical day for enjoying this unusual sport.

> On a lazy, hot summer afternoon in Southern Illinois, when someone jumps out of a lawnchair and hollers, "Let's all go down to the river!" the person is not inviting everyone to join in and sing a chorus or two of Johnny Paycheck's popular Country and Western song. And they're not issuing a general invitation to go witness the Baptists being christened in the creek, either.
>
> 'Going to the river' on a steamy summer Sunday afternoon means something else to my kinfolk and me: a couple of hours of fun and hog-fishing. It may sound like a normal pastime, but it's not. Not when you take into consideration that we'll use no nets, lines, traps, seines, bait, tackle—or for that matter—pigs.
>
> What's left? The cheapest fishing equipment on God's Green Earth. Our hands—as we keep an eye out for Cottonmouth Water Moccasins—and match wits and nerve with wily Carp and Bullhead Catfish who've been lurking in the shallows long enough to weigh sometimes upwards of twenty pounds each.

With this brief opener the reader is pulled into the action, learns about a new and very unusual experience, and in the course of the article is given a lot of practical information, so that by the time the reader finishes the article, he or she would know just exactly how to go about "hogging," even if it's unlikely that the individual will ever actually follow through and try the unusual and sometimes unnerving sport.

Another idea, and one with a national focus that allowed me to target audiences farther removed from the general midwestern region was a piece devoted to hunting for Indian artifacts, another common local interest for those of us who live in the hill country jutting up between the wealth of creeks and rivers that crisscross Southern Illinois.

These waterways were once used as transportation routes by Native Americans who camped on the bluffs where we now live, and left behind arrowheads and implements when they moved on in pursuit of their nomadic life-style. Following a heavy rain, scanning the hillsides and poking at bits of exposed rock with a pointed stick, frequently produces beautiful arrowheads, spear-points, beads, or other small artifacts.

"Arrowhead Hunting: Happ(il)y Hunting Ground" was also published numerous times, and drew the reader into the article by presenting an image most of us have probably seen in cartoons.

> At the mention of the term "Stone Age," many people think of the hirsute, fur-clad cave dweller, lumbering along with a club slung over his shoulder, and the little woman unprotestingly bouncing along behind, towed by her crowning glory.
>
> Many people do not stop to think that our own Native American Indians also dwelled in the Stone Age, creating useful domestic gadgets, tools, and even trinkets and toys from rock.
>
> These items, which are often as valuable as they are beautiful, can, literally, be found in your backyard, if you know how to decide where to look. Hunting for ancient Indian artifacts can be an especially enjoyable and satisfying adventure if you happen to live in an area once frequented by Native American tribes, and if you have a chance to hit-the-bluffs after a sluicing rain, and don't mind dealing with a little mud.
>
> On our acreage, arrowhead hunting becomes a family affair . . .

9.5 Take-Away Value for the Armchair Enthusiast

Beginnings for personal experience wildlife and nature articles are important, for you'll want to draw the reader into the action quickly. I've found that a very workable format for this type of article is to have in the middle reaches of the article a lot of practical information combined with the personal narrative of the experience, along with recreated snatches of dialogue that are appropriate. I like to insert some facts about the topic, ranging from basic to esoteric, to provide take-away knowledge and to give background information to educate the audience.

This can easily be accomplished by researching the specific plant or animal in the encyclopedia, or availing yourself of the lore that can be located in Little Golden Books devoted to such categories as trees, plants, birds, insects, or other topics.

Other possible ways to add related filler to flesh out your true-life experience is to briefly mention the experiences of old-timers, or other outdoorsmen who are serious about the sport, who might have related some incredible yarns, or intriguing "old wives' tales" about either the activity or the wildlife involved.

While the beginning and middle of the manuscript tend to give depth and substance to the true-life wildlife article, the ending is important, too, and in my experience editors seem to show a preference for manuscripts that go "full circle," with the wrap-up paragraph directly linked to the opening hook, to give the article a very finished format so the reader won't flip over to the next page, expecting the piece to continue. The "hogging" article ended with this summation (following the sharing of a few of my recipes that work well for canning the catch, as well as directions for removing the "mud vein"):

> While some people admit to liking the flavor of Carp when the mud vein has been removed, not everyone does. And not everyone will bother to can a "rough," non-game fish and invest the time and effort required to render it into a palatable form for the dinner table.
>
> Within our family, the day's haul is put to good use, as it is with other hog farmers who live along the rivers and creeks. We always have a handy outlet for the catch. Even the laziest old sow will squirm from a muddy wallow when the group returns from the river, dragging burlap bags holding mammoth fish toward the pasture and hollering, "Soooiiiieeee, pig!"
>
> Hogs are smart animals with excellent memories, and from past experience, they know what that means, and they squeal in anticipation as they line up along the electric fence ready to fight over a perfect Sunday snack: fresh Carp.
>
> Hogs love 'em. And that could just be how "hog" fishing got its name.

9.6   Profiting Big from a Wild Sense of Humor

Although the bulk of what various wildlife publications print are serious articles depicting an unusual sport or an unusual treatment of a common outdoor activity, most editors in the field will purchase a good humor manuscript if it's something that their readership can relate to, is focused, to the point, and well-written, amusing, and preferably filler length.

My husband, who is an avid outdoorsman, and I have owned a lot of dogs, and I've found the various mutts excellent material for personal experience articles.

We once had a Blue Tick Coon Hound who was so gangly and homely that I couldn't help laughing each time I saw him. To my astonishment one day I smiled at Towzer, and the dog grinned right back. It seemed like a fluke, but it didn't take long for us to realize that it wasn't a coincidence. Towzer was a grinning coon dog! If we smiled at him he reciprocated by smiling right back.

Our friends knew of our eccentric hound's habits. Strangers did not, however, and Towzer's welcoming grin was sometimes construed for a vicious, soundless snarl, as happened the afternoon he inspired an article entitled "Saved by the Dog," a humor piece that has appeared in quite a number of wildlife publications.

I organized the article to cover the story from Towzer's arrival at our residence to a door-to-door salesman's panicky departure, doing so in approximately 500 words.

"Well, hon, what do you think of him?" My husband asked, his voice proud as he opened the car door.

I looked at the curled up mutt on the floor of the car: speckled, gangling, four months old, and looking for all the world as if he'd been created from mismatched parts left over in a dog factory.

"He's ugly! I—I mean, he's so ugly that he's kind of cute," I tactfully amended.

The narrative then progressed through Towzer's lack of talent, and that he showed a capacity to excel at only the ability to lay in front of the back door so I had to rather rudely disturb him countless times each day to go about my chores.

Each time I nudged him aside, he looked at me, his long ears drooping grudgingly, his eyes soulful, as he unwound his lanky length and lethargically moved aside. I couldn't help laughing. Then one day when I chuckled, he wagged his tail and curled his lips, bearing his teeth in a big smile.

I couldn't believe my eyes. I stared at him. The smile slid from Towzer's face. Puzzled, he cocked his head and peered into my face, his countenance an expression of befuddled hurt.

"It can't be," I muttered. Glancing around, I lowered my voice. "Hey Towzer, smile!" I ordered, and grinned at him.

Wagging with relief, he smiled right back. Twice more I stopped. So did he. Twice more I grinned. He did too!

And so Towzer became known as The Grinning Coon Dog. But fortunately not everyone was privy to his genius, I discovered, when an overly zealous door-to-door salesman arrived just as I'd set about canning a day's harvest from the garden and really didn't relish the interruption at that precise moment.

. . . Regardless, I forced a welcoming smile to my face and walked out to head the salesman off at the gate. As was his custom, after arising to allow me passage, Towzer trailed along at my side.

The balding, perspiring salesman was fumbling in his case for papers and pamphlets describing his wares, as he gave me a breathless greeting. When he was about five feet from me, he hurled the papers like confetti, turned on his heel and bolted for his van, zipping down the lane in a cloud of dust.

Startled, I stared after him, wondering what had gotten into him to convince him to leave in such a hurry.

I leaned down to retrieve the abandoned pamphlets. My face inched down. Towzer's muzzle angled up. And I saw what the salesman had seen: a one hundred and forty pound dog with a full set of uppers and lowers bared into the most ferocious grin I could've ever hope to see.

Towzer grinned even broader when I patted his head and went in to get him a doggie treat. After all, he deserved it, for my afternoon had just been saved by the dog!

Overall the nature, conservation, wildlife, and ecology publications are among the fastest-growing areas of publishing as an increasing number of readers desire to learn more about the great outdoors, even if they do so only from their armchairs. So set out in search of your publishing "game," and by using a camera and typewriter as your "weapons," stalk the markets, then flush out your quarry and bag a few literary trophies you'll be proud to display for the entertainment and edification of others.

CHAPTER
10

Writing for the Paranormal,
Metaphysical, Unusual
Phenomenon, and New Age
Publications

There are a number of magazines devoted to the astrological, metaphysical, and New Age concepts for there is a growing interest in
human experience ranging from the occult to holistic healing
methods.

The paranormal experience magazines run the gamut from those
whose audiences are devotees of astrology, on down to individuals
with interests in psychic phenomena, and those fascinated by the
metaphysical and parapsychology when viewed either as serious
sciences or treated as merely topics of curiosity.

10.1 No Frippery or Tomfoolery Allowed

This category of true-life story writing is not for everyone, as
many people live out their lifetimes without being aware of having
had an unusual event transpire in their lives. But if you have
experienced an unusual phenomenon, or you know of someone who
has, your story, or theirs, could serve as the basis for cracking this
small but thriving market.

A number of the magazines listed in market guides warn writers
up front that they wish to have notarized statements swearing to the
veracity of the manuscripts, and it can facilitate the submission/
acceptance process, if you strive for a professional attitude and
provide this documentation before they have to ask for it. Usually
the fee charged by a notary public is quite small, although worth it,
even though it does cause overhead costs to rise.

10.2   Compensation—In The Great Beyond
       (Beyond Magazines)

Unfortunately, usually within this field the pay is relatively modest. But the writing credits can mount up and it is possible for spin-off deals to come to the author via this avenue, as happened to me following the publication of a precognitive experience in *Fate* magazine when a television producer, who regularly scanned various publications in search of workable ideas for his program, "That's Incredible," contacted me, desiring to film my experience for the enjoyment of their viewing audience.

10.3   Normal Fare for the Paranormal
       Markets

The kinds of articles that are successful in these types of magazines run the gamut. They range from common, everyday situations paralleling *déjà vu*, precognitive dreams, and mental telepathy, to astral projection experiences that most people will never have happen in a lifetime of active living (and probably wouldn't want to), and also encompass such bizarre circumstances as alien encounters, UFO sightings, etcetera.

To feed these markets' insatiable needs with many of them publishing a large number of filler-length first-person accounts each month in addition to feature-length articles, keep in mind that the manuscript's content needn't be *National Enquirer*-shocking, nor of international interest, for it to capture the attention of editors on behalf of their market's targeted readers.

If there's something that has everyone in your area talking, chances are good it will appeal to a magazine readership that thrives on stories a bit out of the ordinary, but down-to-earth enough so that most can conceive of perhaps one day personally experiencing such a situation. This happened when my brother-in-law and several working men returning home after working second shift were talking on their Citizens' Band radios, saw a strange vessel in the sky, and were remarking about it, when suddenly their radios went dead. They pulled off the road along the highway, watched the hovering aircraft with fascinated horror, and stared as it shot out of sight at incredible speed. Returning to their vehicles, they found that their radios had begun working again.

Community knowledge was the case of a life-after-life experience that I became aware of in my hometown, a tiny village on the Canadian border populated by grass roots people who weren't into hoaxes or chicanery.

We all learned of this unusual life experience at least a half dozen years before Raymond Moody wrote his best-selling book excerpting case histories of people he'd interviewed who'd been clinically dead, and were later revived to tell their stories about life-after-death. Some years later, when his book arrived on the scene, residents of my hometown nodded over Moody's book; for his book had a ring of truth as they'd already heard the phenomenon explained by one of our most revered residents.

10.4   Telling It Like It Was

Because it was not my personal experience but another's, I chose third person point-of-view and set out to plot the true-life story so it would, as briefly as possible, share with the readers the exact circumstances as we'd been told by family members who were involved.

The call came to Dr. Lloyd Lofgren, a young family practice physician, as he was wrapping up his day's scheduling at the clinic in a northern Minnesota college town.

Dr. Lofgren had only one patient left to see before he would be free to head home to his wife and family to enjoy a quiet evening seated close to the roaring fireplace in the livingroom, reading the daily paper, as was his nightly ritual.

But the direction of his life changed when the telephone on his desk buzzed. He pressed the button and picked up the receiver.

"Emergency call on line three," his smooth-voiced receptionist said.

When Dr. Lofgren took the call, he recognized the voice on the other end a split second before the speaker provided his identity.

He knew then that he wasn't being contacted by the local hospital staff about a patient on one of the wards who'd taken a turn for the worse and he realized that he faced an arduous trip, through a raging Minnesota blizzard, to be with his widowed mother, Marjorie, in his hometown 120 miles further north.

"Sorry, son," Dr. Dahl, the elderly physician who'd delivered Lloyd almost forty years before, said. "I just admitted your mother to the hospital. She's not going to make it this time. You'd better come right away. I know that the weather's bad—but if you want to see her one last time, you'd better strap on the chains and travel anyway. She won't be here in the morning. . . ."

Lloyd quickly consulted with his last patient, called his wife to sketch in what had transpired, and he set out over the snowpacked, icy highways, made more treacherous by drifts of snow that slanted across the roadway, to see his mother one last time.

He didn't take time to make arrangements for lodging. He could stay at either his mother's home, or with his elderly Aunt Trina, who always welcomed company.

These opening paragraphs have introduced the major characters, set the scene, sketched in the situation, and by mentioning Dr. Lofgren's plans for lodging, laid the groundwork for a plausible ending for the unusual story involving his aunt.

Upon arriving at the hospital, Lloyd assessed the medical situation, phoned his Aunt Trina to check in with her, and then he returned to begin his vigil. With his trained eye he sees signs that death is overtaking his mother, and he plans to stay by her bedside throughout the night so that he can be with her when she passes on.

Dr. Lofgren had been up since before dawn, but weariness overcame him for random moments and his head slumped forward and he dozed. He awoke with a start when his mother thrashed upon the hospital bed. He rushed to her side. Tears stung his eyes when he realized his mother lay moments away from surrendering to death and he anticipated each frenzied movement would become her last.

But, instead the crisis passed. The elderly Mrs. Lofgren's vital signs stabilized, and Lloyd began to dare hope that she would live. It was a medical opinion confirmed when Dr. Dahl made his rounds that morning.

"I should probably call Aunt Trina with the good news," Lloyd said. "But I'm going to stop by her house later on."

"Then let her sleep," Dr. Dahl suggested. "She needs her rest. The news will keep. We'll know more by then anyway."

And so an important decision, but one that seems to reassure the reader about Aunt Trina's well-being, is made.

An hour or two later, Dr. Lofgren was about to depart his mother's room when her eyes flickered open, prompting him to stay.

"How're you feeling, Mom?" he asked, taking her hand.

She tried to smile and sit up, but lacked the strength.

"Much better," she murmured from between dry, cracked lips.

"That's great, Mom. You gave us quite a scare."

"Lloyd . . . I've got to tell you something. I—I died last night."

A jolt of trepidation shot through him. Had something happened to his mother's mind? Had she been so sick that there would be lasting ill effects?

"No, Mom. You're fine. You're going to get better. You didn't die. But you were awfully sick. You probably won't feel like yourself for a few days."

"You don't believe me," she said, her voice tiredly frustrated. "Probably no one will. But Lloyd, I died. And . . . and I came back to life. It was so strange. So very . . . very odd."

In a feeble voice, the woman explained to her son what had happened while he'd stood beside her bed as she thrashed about.

"I felt myself dying right then. And I left my body. I was floating above the bed. I saw you sitting here beside me. Then I was caught up in a . . . a tunnel. It was foggy and I couldn't see well, although I was aware I was moving rapidly toward a bright light in the distance. I knew that I was moving toward something—someone. As I got closer, coming out of the mist, I saw that it was Mama, and with her was Uncle John, and my brother, Leo, who was killed in the Big War. But as I drew nearer to them, they began to retreat. They were upset with me, and they started gesturing for me to go back. I was puzzled. I wanted to be with them. But they said, 'Go back, Marjorie, it's not you we want! Go back—we want Trina.'

"And I came back. . . ." she whispered, finishing her strange account.

Silence spiraled in the quiet room as various machines and monitors softly blipped and hummed.

What his mother had just told him was unlike anything the young physician had ever heard.

"That's quite a story, Mom. But when you're as sick as you were, it's not unusual to hallucinate like that."

"It wasn't a hallucination!" she protested. "Last night I died but came back to life. Now I'm worried about Trina!"

"Well don't worry about her, Mom. She's fine. In fact, I'm going to zip by the bakery, pick up some rolls, then go to Aunt Trina's for coffee. I'll have her call you. Okay?"

Twenty minutes later, clutching a warm and aromatic waxed sack from the bakery, Dr. Lofgren stood on the snow-covered steps of his aunt's home, shivering in the thirty-degree below zero weather. When his aunt didn't respond to his persistent ringing of the doorbell, he withdrew his key ring and found the one required to unlock her home.

Then he discovered why she hadn't come to answer the door.

For during the night, Aunt Trina had died. . . .

10.5   A Dream-Come-True Market

Some people have what are known as precognitive experiences, wherein they have a vivid dream while asleep, and usually within a short period of time, the sequence occurs in reality just as it had progressed while in a dream-state. There are instances where persons entertaining precognitive flashes have tried to avert fires, air disasters, and other headline capturing events, and even regional daily newspapers now commonly report when law enforcement personnel are warned of crimes or pending disasters by persons who've had precognitive dreams. And police, at a loss to solve a crime or locate a missing person will seek the services of a recognized psychic.

If you've ever experienced precognitive phenomena, or a paranormal event, your situation needn't be of sufficient scope to interest the weekly tabloids for you to see it in print, and perhaps even receive an offer to have your story documented for a television viewing audience.

Such was the case for my short filler-length story in *Fate* magazine, "I Dream of Ginny."

My husband sighed as he hung up the telephone after calling around the neighborhood to inquire if they'd heard a dog barking in the woodlands during the past two weeks.

None of them had.

Ginny, our Irish Setter, had been gone from our farm for two weeks. She'd broken loose and trotted off dragging a long dog chain attached to a choke collar. Night after night my husband had searched the immediate area and we had resorted to calling neighbors at points beyond.

"We may as well give up. Face it. She's dead. I've walked up and down creek for miles. She's not going to be able to dig for water with the drought we've had."

I nodded agreement, but I didn't give up. I had such a strong feeling that Ginny wasn't dead, although logic pointed to that fate for a dog dragging a chain in a wild, hilly, rugged terrain, crisscrossed with fallen logs, blackberry brambles, wild rose briars, and saplings that could snare a chain and hold a dog fast. Plus, with the choke chain collar, there was no way she could gnaw her way to freedom. And it would never slip off no matter how thin she got. The collar would shrink as she did.

Six weeks went by. We had long since ceased talking about Ginny. The seventh week after her disappearance, I got up on a sultry Sunday morning in August to get a drink. It was one of the rare days when I could return to bed and sleep late. When I did, I dreamed of Ginny.

I saw her, plain as day, bounding up our lane from the main road. Her long ears flopped, her pink tongue lolled out as she panted and ran. Ginny was brutally thin—every rib showed—and her once glossy red coat was dull and matted with burrs. But she was home—and she was alive!

Then I woke up.

I told my husband about the vivid dream, which had left me feeling oddly unsettled, and he was visibly unimpressed. But:

A half hour later when we got ready to leave to visit relatives, after the screen door banged shut behind us there came a muffled cadence cutting across the lawn. There was Ginny! She was pitifully thin, matted with cockleburs, her long ears flopping, racing joyfully toward us, just as I'd dreamed. Ginny was alive, home, and where she belonged!

We never learned where our Ginny had been, and although we

argued all the possibilities, we finally ended up simply concluding—it was Fate!

The unusual phenomena markets frequently do not insist upon acquiring all rights, and they're willing to settle for one-time rights, although some desire to acquire First North American Rights, so that the author is free to sell the piece elsewhere after its initial publication.

People are more open nowadays to discussing unusual experiences, and if you've heard some incredible, but true, stories, perhaps you're "fated" to find success in this interesting and astonishing area of writing.

CHAPTER
11

Writing for the Humor Markets

To sell humor, you must get serious about being funny.

For me, writing humor is a lot like taking a vacation. It's a dandy place to visit—but I wouldn't care to make my living there—because the marketplace is rather limited. At present, there are only two magazines listed in the humor category that actively solicit personal experience humor stories, as the remainder prefer one-liners and snappy comebacks to market to toastmasters and standup comedians.

The hidden humor market is a lot bigger, as many general publications, not the least of which is *Reader's Digest*, use a great deal of true-life humor. Some trade journals and fraternal organizations, which may not be listed in *Writer's Market*, use humor as well. These trade and fraternal publications may not specify humor as among their needs, but in my experience, I've almost always connected when I sent off a short humor manuscript that was dead-center to their audience's interest.

11.1 Making Funny Money

The various markets using humor have pay rates as diverse as their areas of appeal. But even if the checks are not large, be aware that there is a certain satisfaction in knowing that you're giving many people a good laugh to brighten what may be a dismal day.

To find success you must come up with viable ideas and then craft your manuscript carefully, keeping your targeted audience in mind. You must not settle for less than your best, because to find success it's necessary that your manuscript be funnier than the works of the cut-ups competing against you in the editor's slushpile.

Writing humor may seem like a lighthearted occupation, but it's actually darned hard work, some of the most challenging writing there is.

Editors at most magazines and newspapers see a lot of humor. The somber fact is that what most see simply is not funny. There may be a thigh-slapper of a line here or there but the remainder of the manuscript is boring. The focus isn't sharp because the experience hasn't been "well plotted." Or the delivery isn't punchy. And lack of originality is a sure kiss-of-death. Familiarity of treatment breeds automatic rejection.

11.2   Some Secrets to Selling Humor

The secret to selling humor is to study the markets and key submissions to publications most likely to respond favorably because the amusing manuscript will hit their audience dead center.

The *Angus Journal* is a highly technical publication that goes out to people who raise Black or Red Angus beef cattle as a cash crop. I decided to change the generic "steer" to a "Black Angus steer" (with a nod to "literary license") and I sent off the manuscript "You Are What You Eat?!," about a true-life "anorexic" steer we'd once had on the farm, and the editor accepted it by return mail.

Cattlemen who feed-out livestock want them to go from birth to market-weight as quickly as possible. With Calfy, that wasn't the case.

The fellows at the farm supply store would never guess, judging by our feed purchases, that we have animals afflicted with the severe psychological disturbances that cause the dread modern maladies: eating disorders.

Granted, we had no trouble with the swine. Those dudes were very single-minded about it all and protected their hoggy reputations. As long as there was corn in the feeder they were content to do their thing: PIG OUT!

Over the years, the cattle created chaos with their oddities. Calfy was the first. An avowed glutton with an insatiable appetite, who had only the goats, Gottfried and Hilda, for social contacts, he ate anything and everything. Hay. Corn. Molasses. Leaves. Wood bark. Ashes. Dirt. Rubber hoses. Tin cans.

Anything in Calfy's path—and even tidbits he had to detour to find—he was willing to try. With time, and the arrival of a connoisseur's temperament, Calfy's tastes grew ever more exotic and expensive. He'd scarf down barbed wire, can lids, baler twine, and any stray bit of rubbish that he could locate to sate his perverse desire for JUNK FOOD.

Soon Calfy was joined by Axehandle, a narrow-hipped beast, who wasn't living up to his name, and knew that the faster he grew, the sooner he'd keep an appointment with the Grim Packer. With a desperate need to control the situation and his life, as is common with the disorder, Axehandle developed anorexia nervosa.

Pour corn in the feeder? He'd look ill and walk away. Not hungry. Put hay in the manger? He didn't bother to investigate. "Not hungry," the switch of his long, skinny tail seemed to say. Pour molasses on the oats? That brought an indignant stare. What were we trying to do? Get him off his diet?!

Opinion or Editorial pages can be a good place for a humorist to break into print with a personal experience story. Most Op-Ed editors find humor makes appealing copy, especially if there's a funny local tie-in or the idea is extremely universal in appeal.

I have sold "Confessions of a Tooth Fairy" numerous times, because it's a role almost any woman who finds herself a mother eventually must fill. Two other strong sellers to the Op-Ed or Sunday Supplement sections nationwide, "Close Encounters of the Safety Cap Kind" and "Consumer Profile-RFD," (sparked by "junk mail"), and "Once A Year Witch," a piece championing the rights of those of us who, faced with the challenge of costuming kiddies for Halloween, quite frankly, resent the women who take a roll of Charmin' and transform a child into Cinderella. Or create a Tin Man by crocheting Brillo pads in their spare moments.

Humor writers should seek to develop a strong, clear, individual writing style, and when possible go for repeat sales with the editors who like their style and content.

Some years ago, one editor referred to me as "The Erma Bombeck of the Barn Yard," because I sold a great deal of rural-oriented humor because I examined my daily life and consciously looked for funny episodes to turn into humor articles. I contributed regularly to *Farm Wife News*, later called *Country Woman*, and I retained rights so that I resold many of the articles and compiled them into an anthology of humor pieces.

Just as Erma Bombeck writes humor based on her personal experiences in suburbia, so I have ideas sparked by my life-style as a country dweller. It helps, of course, if you have a funny husband, amusing children, hilarious pets and eccentric neighbors. I have not always been so blessed, nor, probably, has Erma Bombeck, so we make do with what material's available, and so can you.

11.3   Serious Aspects About Creating Light Writing

Making it as a humor writer isn't a case of having hilarious things happen to you every day; it's actually a matter of transforming common situations into amusing universal episodes that others can relate to, laughing as they recognize similar events and reactions in their own lives.

Don't take it for granted that the reader will "get" the humor of a manuscript, or find a piece funny, just because you do. What is common in the USA, like "Tooth Fairies," is a phenomenon unheard of, say, in Denmark, where baby's first tooth is mounted into a gold setting to be worn as a ring. Therefore, while many humor pieces sold in the United States can be marketed to overseas publications, obviously some humor pieces will lose something in the translation.

When coming up with ideas, I've found that there's generally a very fine line between anger and humor. I first discovered a capacity to be funny shortly after we moved to an eighty-acre farm in Southern Illinois, and my husband began subjecting me to an increasingly odd menagerie of pets. In telling friends about my woes, instead of sympathizing with me, they began to giggle, and I realized that instead of being constantly perturbed by the antics of the eccentric critters, I could profit from their presence, as I wrote pieces like:

The Goats That Got My Goat
Why I have a Foul/Fowl Temper
Don't be Bored/Boared—Raise Hogs!
Modern Farming Methods Going to the Dogs
How to Raise Ducks, By Quacky
Mudwhumpers Who've Muddied Up My Life, etcetera.

Admittedly, the titles are pure corn, but what else would you want when you're writing humor articles that are basically agriculturally oriented for a largely rural audience?

They were the kinds of titles that editors who accepted them saw as workable blurb lines. I believe if the title fits—use it, because I feel it can add extra sales appeal, because it encourages the editor to think in terms of accompanying illustrations.

11.4   Writing Good Humor Is No Joking Matter

Writing humor is not easy. Sometimes it's not even fun. It certainly demands discipline, sometimes in unusual amounts, compared to writing in other areas. Successful humor writers, most especially columnists, cannot wait for "The Muse" nor for a time in which they happen to be feeling especially funny. They must examine the world around them and the realm of personal experience for workable ideas. Humor must be worked at—even forced out—just like any other kind of writing. Writing salable humor is a strenuous undertaking because it sometimes requires extensive rewriting to make a manuscript really work.

The first stage for writing humor—the rough draft—is where everything having to do with the topic should be poured onto the page. Then comes the most important labor, that of mercilessly editing what's been written. *And if it's not funny—take it out!* Cross out the material, yes, but please, do yourself a favor and don't discard it. It could be very useful at another time and work beautifully in a different humor piece.

11.5   Computer Generated Laughs

Writers who work with word processors may have to revise their working methods when they draft humor pieces on computer disk because the punch of a button can send some great lines into computer never-never land, lost forever.

My personal method in using a computer is to copy sections to be deleted into their own files. Or, at the very least, to print out hard copy on paper, so that there's a written record of the abandoned copy. That way, it spares me the frustration of having deleted a few lines only to realize that they were actually good, and then being unable to recreate the succinct phrasing that captured the essence so nicely initially. If a neat turn-of-phrase exists somewhere on paper, or has been copied into a temporary reserve file on disk, it can always be keyed back in. Delete in haste—and you'll very likely repent at leisure.

Ruthless editing increases the chances for acceptance when excess verbiage is trimmed away before an editor sees it. Most magazines and newspapers that use humor have a limited amount of space—generally it qualifies as filler material—so the shorter the manuscript copy the better.

11.6   Polishing the Punch Lines

Sustaining a pleasing amount of humor, which registers almost like a measurable commodity, is attained through fine-tuning the manuscript. So organization is important, as it gives continuity and something very important, known in the business as "timing," which can occur on the page as well as in live performances.

Most true-life incidents are not funny if you relate them exactly as they took place. The essence of humor is actually extracted through the careful selection for inclusion, and equally careful omission, from the basic true situation. Whether it's called "literary license," "embroidering the truth," or "telling lies for fun and profit," exaggeration is a requisite for creating a satisfying humor article.

11.7   The Eyes Have It

What is forgiven by the ear will not be overlooked by the eye. When we talk we can ramble, stutter, make mistakes, and we're forgiven if our train of thought bounces back and forth a little. But in humor articles we must carefully "funnel" information so that the entire piece flows smoothly from beginning to end so that there are no choppy, bumpy areas.

11.8   Getting Started

As with other areas of personal experience writing, when it comes to humor structure is the name of the game, so give the topic a lot of thought. Select an angle that you plan to use. Write notes to yourself. Jot down funny phrases. List plays on words. Before you begin writing compile your notes, lay them out in the order that they should appear, and you have an instant outline to follow as you draft your personal experience humor piece.

11.9   Creating Generic Entertainment

I feel that humor writers should avoid using actual given names because this throws up a barrier, reminding the reader that he or she does not really know the person, and it shatters the rapport between humor writer and reader. It breaks the spell as it reminds the reader that the universal situation happened to someone else. And then again, sometimes the people who may spark the funniest ideas in us as we encounter them as we go about living, could view it as an invasion of privacy, or being held up for ridicule; it's a wise idea to select clever tag names so that your reader can relate to the humor piece on a personal level, mentally filling in their own family's identity in the cameo roles in the published piece.

In "Confessions of a Tooth Fairy," I avoided gender references and I always gave the child involved a "generic" tag, and also structurally borrowed from the readily recognizable "Mission: IMPOSSIBLE" format from the once-popular television show.

Somewhere between the medulla and cerebellum, a tiny portion of the brain lies dormant in the female species, until the woman is confronted by the first newly lost tooth in the family. The sight of the little chunk of used calcium activates the ability. The message from this special brain center is always delivered in a nasty, sing-songy, slightly gloating, elfin voice, with all the charm and compassion of a dentist's drill.

"This is a mission of Top Secret," the badgering voice rubs in. "As a mother, you have no choice in the matter. You WILL accept the mission whether you want to or not. You are hereby directed to sneak upon the sleeping child, remove the heavily guarded tooth from beneath the pillow, and in its place substitute money. Under the cover of darkness you will return, undetected, to your bed, but only after you have secreted the tooth in a safe place to preserve it for all posterity." The tiny internal voice now becomes disparaging. "And if you flub up and are detected in the execution of this operation, you are to disavow any knowledge whatsoever of a mission, shield the Tooth Fairy legend with your life, or your child's belief in the Tooth Fairy will instantly self-destruct."

Talk of the Tooth Fairy ran rampant that evening. Finally the clock strikes midnight, and all is quiet except for spousal snoring and the gnawing of mice who are not stereotypically quiet. Like a spirit from the grave I arise and go forth, gliding flat-footed across the floor to keep from making noise or stumbling over every stick of furniture in the house as I attempt to see Operation: Swipe-A-Tooth through to completion.

The operation is jinxed from the start. A door hinge that habitually opens with a soft hush, whines like banshees from the pits of hell. The next one opens too easily and cracks against the wall creating a noise like the Clap of Doom. My breath, once not even audible, rattles and wheezes with every expulsion, and floorboards once silent groan and creak with every step.

Through the maternal cacophony the Keeper-of-the-Tooth sleeps on, visions of things that go clink-in-the-bank (not decay—causing sugar plums) dancing in the Little Loser's head.

Furtively I slide a dishpan hand under the pillow. SNAP! The Endentulous Kid pulling Guard Duty, jerks to attention. "Who goes there? MOM! What ARE you DOING?" The chagrined kid hisses, through clenched—and missing—teeth. "Go back to bed! You'll scare the Tooth Fairy away!"

And in the case of a farm humor article, "Don't Get Bored/Boared, Raise Hogs!" I gave our livestock embellishments to what were actually their names.

Zipping from the barn I saw a six-hundred-and-fifty-pound boar disappear over a rise, with my six-foot-three, two-hundred pound spouse in hot pursuit. Cedric ran as if his life depended on it. And being as our destination was the livestock auction—it did.

The farmer lunged. Cedric squealed. "Hurry!" The Farmer-in-Residence bellowed. "I can't hold him forever!"

And he couldn't. A terrific Cedric was off and running while I chugged toward the farmer who stood shaking his head in dismay.

"I'm going to catch him by the tail," the In-Home Gentleman Farmer decided. "You slip some binder twine around his hind leg." He handed it to me and we sprinted off after the Cross-Country Porker.

Cedric was hoping for survival of the FATTEST. But it was

actually a matter of survival of the FASTEST. And Cedric's get-up-and-go was soon gone. He circled back, panting, his tongue hanging out, to trot past Lulubelle, the Harlot of the Hog Lot.

Flushing and simpering, she batted her stubby eyelashes, certain her paramour's breathless demeanor was in response to her cheesecake posing beside the swill. Passion was not foremost in Cedric's mind. The hog had lust all right—a lust to LIVE.

"I've got him!" The Farmer whooped. Cedric howled. I hot-footed it across the pasture and when Cedric spotted the tie-that-binds, his adrenaline surged.

My long, lean spouse clung to the porker's curly tail, and he planted his feet, hauling downhill. His bootheels dug furrows each time Cedric inched ahead, pawing for traction.

I tried to lasso a pre-pickled pork hock, as the Gargantuan Gigolo tapdanced in terror. Finally the twine settled around a plump ankle. I started to pull it tight.

"ARRRRRRGGGHH!" Came the mortal duet.

The Farmer flew nose-over-teakettle down the knoll as Cedric catapulted up the hill. Dazed, the Farmer landed: bottom down, feet up, hands still clenching six inches of bristly boar-tail.

"What'd you let him go for?" The Farmer cried as Cedric streaked across the pasture, twine a-flapping. Pitching the scruffy tail into the bushes, with a yell The Farmer took off after the tail-less Cedric, who was probably hoping to pass for a Guinea Pig so he could become a pet and escape his fate as a porkburger.

11.10   Do unto Others

My rural-oriented pieces are actually *true*, with very little literary license, except to tell the story by giving animals human tendencies and motivations.

The Farmer knows he's pulled some good ones on me over the years, but I try to write humor so that even when folks laugh over what's gone on here at "Sow's Ear Acres" The Farmer still has his self-respect. I feel that no acceptance check is worth it if I put a price tag on someone else's self-image, privacy, or seem to ignore the potential to cause hurt feelings in my attempt to make a humorous point and earn a few bucks. I always try to "do unto others as I would have them do unto me." Destructive, derogatory, sarcastic treatments really aren't funny, and generally they result in the humorist winning scorn instead of success.

11.11   To Thine Own Self

But when it comes to earning a laugh, I'm certainly not against taking a poke at myself, as I did in "Consumer Profiles—RFD," as I invite readers to recognize the same situation in their lives and laugh along with me.

It's hard to believe that only a few short years ago, I coveted my neighbors' mailboxes. Oh, how envious I was of all their samples, opinion polls, luxurious offers, and heart-rending solicitations.

Then, one fine day, I got my first bulk-rate envelope. "IMPORTANT! DO NOT DESTROY!" the envelope warned in bold red letters.

Destroy it? Fie! I planned on framing it.

Needless to say, I was disappointed to learn that the contents were of such importance that the mailers hadn't bothered to seal the envelope and the contents had been consumed by the bowels of the United States Postal System.

But, I contented myself, it WAS a start. . . .

Maybe I wasn't well-clothed enough to make the best-dressed list. Nor sloppy enough to make the worst-dressed list. Nor well-heeled enough to make the richest-list. But I possessed a name and a new mailbox, all that I needed to win a slot on someone's mailing list.

Flyers came flocking in. Not only to me, but to some people by the names of "Occupant," "Resident," and "Postal Patron." I was such a Junky For Mail that I opened not only my mail but theirs, too.

The first batch offered glorious trips. Not particularly appropriate for a farm family responsible for the daily care of critters. But it was the thought behind the invitation that counted, and I was touched.

There was more. Neato appliance offers. Tempting cutlery to consider. Brilliant, dazzling towels. And myriad other lavish and lovely goodies. It was simple. All I needed to do, they explained in titillating terms, was send in the postage paid card, and pay the "EASY TERMS"—concealed in microscopic print—for the rest of my earthly existence.

Then, alas, some rat-fink must've blown the whistle on me.

The luxury offers abruptly stopped. And in their place I got a freebie can of deodorant. Various lending institutions, who seemed to know something about my financial situation that I did not, were telling me to cheer up. They made it compassionately clear that I wasn't too bad a risk for THEM. If I'd just scribble my name on the dotted line—they'd get me out of debt F-A-S-T.

What they were neither cheerful nor compassionate about, was the fact, in tiny print, that if I ever failed to make the EASY PAYMENTS, a humanized King Kong would arrive via Express Mail to break both of my arms so that I'd never be able to sign on a dotted line again.

Then our fiscal picture changed again, because suddenly I was considered worth putting-the-touch on. Deadbeat mail beat a hasty retreat. Solicitations waltzed right in. The poster children were so skinny that there was plenty of room left in the mailbox for newspapers, magazines and seed catalogs. The timing was great and the pictures most effective. It was the first time I lost weight between Thanksgiving and New Year's. I was planning on writing a book, promoting a new diet plan, with the proceeds to go to a favorite charity for starving children.

But before I got around to it, starving children got their fill of me, and religious organizations began vying for my attention, my soul, but most especially, my money. I truly appreciated their good intentions, although I'll admit that I was concerned that all of their prayers on my behalf would be posted in the wrong account, because they consistently spelled my name wrong.

En masse the clergy washed their hands of me. . . .

But, that was okay, because following their barrage I dealt with cheese promotions, dating club promotionals, and even sex toy catalogs and sundry other bulk-rate offers including various get-rich-quick schemes. These are all direct mail offers for items that most people become accustomed to receiving.

After sustaining the pace, I wanted to wrap the piece up quickly, but in what would be an unexpected manner.

. . . I know that if I ever get hauled in by the police, I'll be well advised not to ask my mail carrier to step forward and serve as a character witness, for gauging by the contents of my mail over the years, the perplexed mailman would probably scratch his head and sum me up as:

"Well, I'd have to say that she's a financially precarious, luxury-lover, with B.O., who feels sorry for starving kids, passed up

religion for sex, is going to make it big with a get-rich-quick
scheme that's going to save her from the loan sharks. And she likes
cheese."

11.12   And to All Things Great and Small

Word selection is of utmost importance as vivid word pictures are
created to make the reader form a mental image, and it works well to
give animals human traits and tendencies. Such was the case in
"Surrogate Motherhood, Extended Families, and Other Sociologi-
cally Aware Critters We Have Known," based on the true-life experience of when a mallard duck hatched out eighteen eggs, at the same
time a stupid turkey was derelict in her maternal duties.

> Daddy Drake did-his-stuff and Mama Duck staked out Squatter's
> Rights near the back door where she hid on her eggs, and might've
> even gone unnoticed in the thicket of brush had she had the
> presence of mind to keep-her-quack shut.
>   Mama Duck hatched her brood the same day that one of the
> Moronic Turkeys abdicated the nest, abandoning the sole egg,
> which, in the fracas cracked open to immediately hatch an orphan.

We actually did move the turkey "peep" over to Ma Duck's residence, figuring she had enough maternal instinct to go around.

> It worked like a charm. The gangly, long-toed, gawky little critter
> cuddled up to the web-footed, long-billed Mama Mallard, al-
> though by week's end he had stooped to fit under her wing.
>   Possessing looks that only a mother could love, the little turk
> worked tirelessly to win Mama Duck's approval, up to, and includ-
> ing, unsuccessful and nearly-disastrous dips in the pond.
>   Meanwhile, Mama Duck's neighbor, a loose-moraled and lacka-
> daisical duck, with no interest nor talent for nurturing young,
> hatched one egg and wandered away from her responsibility.
>   Perhaps a desire for penance resulted in Mama Turkey moving in
> to atone for her transgressions, as she volunteered to rear the little
> ducky while its biological mother waddled around in search of the
> good life and wild times as Feather Floozy began to hang around in
> dim-lit barns.

Laughter really is good medicine, and writing humor can be healthy for your career. So if there's a source of irritation in your life, give it a second look, and decide if the personal experience has the humorous capacity required to make the leap from pet peeve to profitable publishing venture.

CHAPTER
12

Writing the True-Crime, Police Procedural Detective Story

An area of personal experience writing, where you wish *not* to have the event in your own life, is the true-crime or police procedural detective story.

Murder is on the increase, even in rural areas, and that means that there are an increasing number of true-life stories to explore, as another's loss of life can represent compensation to you as a writer.

12.1 What Editors Want

Many times, however, a local murder is an open and shut case as soon as the homicide investigators arrive and the several magazines that publish true crime articles are not interested in stories where the perpetrator's identity is established almost as soon as the victim's corpse is discovered—unless the crime is extraordinarily grisly or there are extenuating background circumstances that will fascinate the readership.

Although they will publish "crimes of passion" stories, most police procedural magazines want stories where at least twenty-four hours elapses, preferably longer, so the time span involved allows for more sophisticated police work, a wider cast of suspects, and results in expanded "plotting" of the true experience episode.

Ideally the factual action calls into play the execution of lab work and high-tech analysis techniques that will impress the reader and make it increasingly difficult for a layman to dare to think that he or she can get away with "the perfect crime" as they're left in awe by the discovery techniques that allow for tiny, awe-inspiring clues providing irrefutable evidence that leads directly to the culprit.

12.2 How to Give It to Them

The true-crime story usually opens with the discovery of a body, or bodies, and frequently these lead paragraphs are composed in such a way that an average reader can relate to stumbling over a corpse so unexpectedly, and becoming personally involved in a homicide investigation.

The writing style should be descriptive in order to set the scene, create a mood, and vividly cameo the character types of the various people involved from the commission of the crime, discovery of bodies, through the investigation, on down to solving the crime, wrapping up with the prosecuting and defense attorneys, and even the judge who presides and hands out the eventual prison sentence.

> It had been an average day for the waitress in a downtown Indianapolis restaurant and her apron pocket was jingling with tip money when she turned her station over to the waitress coming on-shift.
>
> Exhaust fans from the restaurant's kitchen vented delicious aromas into the general area, but as the firm's employee crossed a nearby parking lot, nothing could override the stench that hung in the vicinity. Angry green-blue blowflies, filling the air with a tenacious buzzing, hovered around a Lincoln Continental with out-of-state plates.
>
> The waitress, accustomed to temporarily memorizing faces and seating-places, realized that the same car had been sitting in the lot for—how long? One day? Two? Maybe even three?
>
> She knew something wasn't right. And she made it her business to contact authorities so that they could investigate and discover exactly what was wrong.

Readers, who want to be right in the thick of things, also wish to become acquainted with the principal players in the homicide investigation, so they feel as if they're "looking over the shoulder" of those who are at the scene.

Evidence found in the parking lot convinced Police Department homicide investigator Craig Converse that something was seriously amiss, and he called in a crime scene squad to properly handle the scene and to record the episode on videotape.

"We felt there was a strong possibility that there was at least one body in the trunk of the car," he said, to explain his professional judgment call.

It took the investigators about four minutes to pry the trunk lid open, and once that was accomplished, they discovered a quilt shielding decomposing bodies that were covered with constantly shifting larvae as they writhed onward in the hatching process.

To avoid a public spectacle, authorities towed the roomy Lincoln Continental containing its macabre cargo to the police morgue where the bodies were removed and layers of maggots washed away so that the pathologists could search for their grim discoveries.

There would be no need to spend hours of legwork striving to locate the murder implements, for the killer's weapons of choice were also contained in the trunk: a wrench, a pipe, and the scissors still imbedded in the victim's chest cavity, as well as bloody coveralls, clothing commonly worn by farmers across the Midwest, as well as plastic bags containing brain matter.

12.3　Collecting the Facts

It's the writer's job to compile information and this can be done from a variety of sources: newspapers, radio reports (a tape recorder is handy), television coverage (a VCR is valuable), and interviews with law enforcement personnel, court transcripts, etcetera.

Obviously from the above true-life example, if you're the queasy type, writing true-crime might be difficult for you, because the "gory details" are stock-in-trade and it helps if in addition to writing talent you possess a cast-iron stomach and the ability not to dwell too much upon the morbid circumstances confided in you after you've finished processing the crime story for the reading public. It's not worth the financial rewards to tamper with your own personal serenity and risk your own good emotional health for the sake of a good story.

12.4   Naming Names

People want to know who played a part in the unfolding true-life drama and when an article has regional interest, readers in that area can be counted upon to search for familiar names, so use as many as possible, in the appropriate context.

> "Any one of the multiple injuries to Ivy Welch, Forest Janes, and Una Janes could have resulted in their deaths," said Dr. Michael Clark, as he explained the work of the team comprised of three doctors who assisted one another, with Clark the lead pathologist for 93-year-old Ivy Welch's investigation. "For us a triple homicide is an extremely unusual situation. Her throat was cut at least five times. There may have been more. It was hard to sort out how many cuts because of body decomposition."

There are almost always two sides to every story, and while the authorities, who are experts in their fields can offer a great deal to aid the understanding of a crime, personal contacts, area residents, and people close to the families of the victim or the suspect (if an interview can be safely and tactfully arranged), may inject the conflict and human interest that can convince an editor to buy. It's a good idea to use a written release as well as to record the conversation, with a preamble stated on tape that the interviewee understands that he or she is granting rights for you to use as you will in the publishing industry. Giving one dollar in return for rights and considerations can also help protect your interests as the author.

> Mary "Rusty" Kirkham, Ronald Jane's first cousin, believes he was forced into the act. "I think this situation was brought on by aggravation from Frosty Janes. He couldn't say a good word about the boy."
>
> Kirkham then related the content of an April 1990 phone call with Forest that confirmed her suspicions Ron was mentally abused by her uncle who was his adoptive father.
>
> "I called Forest to tell him I couldn't return Ron to their farm, and asked him to retrieve the boy. He said to "tell the son-of-a-bitch to walk home."
>
> "I said, 'Frosty, it's freezing. He'll freeze to death.' " He then said, "He'll never come back here again or I'll kill the SOB."

Another family friend, Edna Cooley, who'd been Una's closest friend and neighbor for over forty years agreed with Kirkham.

"Una really loved Ronny. There wasn't anything she wouldn't have done for Ronny. But he couldn't do anything to suit Frosty and the boy tried to please his father. I think it was hatred and jealousy of how Ron and his mother interacted. I think it (the killings) was all brought on by his father."

"Throughout the years I have known Ron, he has always been a friend. I think there must be more to this," said the Rev. Bill Carter of Faith Builders Church, referring to the irrational, one-time act of homicidal violence.

12.5   Justice in Progress

The true-crime magazines that are published regularly do not insist on totally wrapped-up cases, as they will print pieces that are at various stages of the legal process. Some care must be taken in crafting true-life crime stories that are not 100 percent complete when an article is printed. The manuscript should use qualifying words, such as the "alleged killer," since the "jury is still out" about establishing guilt. However, after a suspect is brought to trial, or if a confession occurs as it did in the above, it's acceptable to use "the convicted killer" or "the confessed murderer" without worrying about trampling on another's civil rights.

Courtroom scenes make riveting reading in the true-crime story, and readers want to get a fix on both the prosecution and the defense so they can envision how they sparred in the courtroom drama.

Ron Janes began showing his questioners a picture in Forest Janes's wallet. "This is my dad's billfold," he said in a husky, choked voice as he produced the item from his pocket. His trembling hands held aloft a picture pinched between his fingers. "There's his baby boy that he was proud of. And I killed him. . . ."

Then the confessed murderer began to brokenly cry.

Defense Attorney L. Stanton Dotson quietly cleared his voice. "I'd like the record to show that through the last part of the testimony he was crying," Dotson requested of Fifth Judicial Circuit Judge Paul Komada, who was hearing the case in the Coles County, Illinois, courthouse.

"Fine, Judge," retorted Assistant Attorney General Richard Schwind, in another of the outbursts of emotion that colored the day's hearing. "But I'd like for the record to also show that he was concerned about getting his cigarettes and another cup of coffee."

Writing stories after the perpetrator has been sent to the slammer can result in more helpful details in the writing of that specific crime story. But taking your time can also result in someone else beating you to the punch by sending the editor their compilation of the same crime and getting the acceptance that might've been yours.

Regardless, trial transcripts and court records can become valuable research tools for developing the total story. And if in researching a case-in-progress you uncover a lot of really interesting data, with unusual motivations and intriguing personalities in conflict, you might discover that you have not only enough to write a good, true-life story for the magazines, but could have sufficient material to warrant doing a full-length, true-crime book, as I am now doing with Ronald Janes's story, as I consult with the defense attorney, the confessed killer, and others, digging back to bring in shaping forces and long ago events that led to the brutal slayings. The book does not attempt to excuse the confessed killer from his heinous crime when he killed his adoptive mother, father, and maternal grandmother, but by bringing to light the years of abuse, the full story that goes beyond what's allowed into the courtroom can shed some light, and point out the unfortunate shared culpability, in the story that comprises the true-life drama to be told in my working title book, "Sins of the Father."

True-crime writing for the magazines can be a nice bread-and-butter market, but if a situation (and it needn't always be a murder) can result in a literary property that can be sold in one of the booming areas of the industry, with many of these nonfiction titles going on to attain best-seller status, and sometimes even garner movie deals, so much the better.

12.6   Plea Bargaining for Pictures

True-crime magazines are a market where accompanying pictures should be considered a necessity. And there are several ways to go about providing them. If you have a professional quality 35mm camera, and possess an eye for detail and photographic arrangement, you can take the pictures yourself.

Or, if you've managed to have a cordial relationship with the families of the victim and the suspect, you might be able to persuade them to give you copies of family pictures.

Newspapers have usually sent reporters to shoot the scene, and more pictures will have been snapped than will have been published, so it's frequently possible to purchase rights to workable photos. Make sure as you're dickering, though, that the people involved realize that you're aiming for success in magazines that have modest pay scales, so that you can't afford to remit photo rights fees that just could add up to what you'd hope to see in payment.

A good bargaining point is to appeal to the photographer's ego and career goals by bringing up the fact that if your piece is accepted for print, he or she will get the photographer's credits in a national magazine, and that this can look nice in his or her professional résumé.

So stalk the true-crime markets like a serial killer and then be ready to absolutely slay the editorial staff with your prose, your pictures, and your professional attention to accuracy and detail.

CHAPTER
13

Writing for the Consenting Adult/Men's Magazines

There are quite a number of adult publications ranging from the lavishly printed skin publications, on down to the poorly produced pink-sleaze productions, that use "true-life" stories—either factual or fictional—with no one terribly concerned which is which, for editors admit it's not up to them to say whether a story is actually true or not.

13.1   A Look at a (Very Revealing) Hidden Market

The "consenting adults" publications constitute a sizable but often hidden market, both literally and figuratively, because many of the magazines, due to local obscenity laws, are sold at magazine stores and convenience outlets only from their repository beneath the counter when clerks dispense them to customers who are age twenty-one or older. They can't be on the racks in plain sight. And in market directories for writers not all players in the erotica category make public appearances, either.

In large cities one can find a wide variety of these publications alongside books, videos, and sex toys, at adult bookstores that cater to salacious material of interest to the over–twenty-one set, with everything available under one roof. The publications are usually very high priced considering that payment tendered to free-lance writers is frequently among the lowest in the business.

13.2   The Lexicon of Lust

The language of lust represents a lexicon that most authors will be uncomfortable using because while in confession and romance-oriented magazines poetry and even flowery euphemisms are allowed, this is not so in the consenting adults publications. In these periodicals, four-letter words and crude expressions, vulgar terms and graphic acts that average people might consider perversions, not only abound but are required if you hope to place your work with these publications.

13.3   The Basic Slant

Even though the style and content is inarguably raw, the focus and guidelines differ greatly among the hide-under-the-counter magazines, and the area of distribution has bearing on this because there are a lot of no-no's (taboo acts) for a writer interested in crafting turn-on stories for the magazines that are sold not only in the United States but also in Canada. A few such strictures include mentioning no characters under age nineteen, no force, violence, bondage and discipline, domination, illegal drugs, bestiality, etcetera.

Writers who, having an idea of what the consenting adults magazines want, and are still interested in exploring the erotica markets, should gather editorial office addresses from the masthead pages of publications that print the kind of material they wish to write and send a self-addressed, stamped envelope requesting current guidelines from the editor.

Until recently, writers who felt comfortable detailing extremely graphic erotic encounters on the printed page, in first-person viewpoint under the guise of true-life experiences in letter form, could earn steady money as purveyors of earthy passion.

But because the magazines have had so many subscribers writing in offering their experiences for free as a recession deepened, many publications no longer buy free-lance work for the turn-on letters section. The pay rates, generally very low compared to other fields of writing, will not allow any writer to quit his or her day job although they'll probably take care of postage overhead.

In some of the more diversified men's skin magazines there is also a need for the first-person fictional "confession" story, usually from the male point-of-view, detailing a lusty, erotic encounter with a wanton, willing woman. Pay is significantly better for these manuscripts but content leans heavily toward nonstop sexual action, and for some writers a desired professional satisfaction is lacking even though they might've easily found a slot in the editor's regular stable.

13.4   Points for Professionals to Ponder

In my years as an instructor for Writer's Digest School, I've had a working relationship with a number of students who made respectable money writing full-length erotica for the consenting adult markets. The money was nice, they admitted, but to a one, all of the students have expressed a desire for something more. Interestingly enough, although they were successful in the erotic field, none of the writers felt as if he was "a real writer" because he hadn't cracked the respectable markets, those places where one could be proud to show the printed piece to friends and family.

In addition, the hard-working, talented students feared (correctly) that in writing porn they'd picked up bad habits that were preventing them from finding success in general magazines. Once accustomed to structuring around sexual escapades, it was like having a whole new vista opened up for them to explore when they studied other structural elements of fiction writing and they matured markedly and went on to sell in the markets where they really wanted to produce.

In addition to the problem of feeling a lack of professional worth, even as credits amass in the consenting adult field at an astonishing rate, the truth is that these credits are valueless. Agents and editors outside this specialized area of publishing do not consider these credits valid, and claiming to having written five hundred "turn-on" letters in a sizzling sexually-oriented magazine won't open any doors to further your career.

Many people believe it's easy to succeed at writing porn, that anyone can write salable sleaze. But those who've done it know that it, too, is hard work, and for an author willing to expend that kind of effort it might be a wise career choice to craft manuscripts in an area where you can have good public exposure, respectable, recognized credits, decent pay, retain some salable subsidiary rights, and follow a logical and professional game plan to further your goals toward enduring career development.

PSYCHOLOGICAL AND PROFESSIONAL POTPOURRI

———

CHAPTER
14

Time to Write—A Do-It-Yourself Project

It's difficult to be a writer trying to cram a career into a twenty-four hour day yet not shortchange those near and dear as we strive to supplement our incomes and earn a place in publishing.

What most authors could use is an efficiency expert. But most authors can't afford the services of such an analyst. However, every author can make use of do-it-yourself methods to budget time and identify problem areas of waste and misappropriation.

A lot of folks spend more time contemplating a chore than they would spend performing the task. A tangible work schedule, whether written on a notepad, or chalked daily on a small blackboard located in a prominent place, can help eliminate this problem because the day's needs are lined up like stepping stones to success, a pathway that merges personal responsibilities and professional obligations.

14.1 The Wonder of Work Lists

A work schedule can be as simple or complex as you like. My personal daily list is unstructured. This list on the steno pad reminds me of special tasks: bake cookies for the church bazaar, dress the kids in green (I once got red-faced sending my children to school on Saint Patrick's Day without appropriate attire), call the dentist, check on an elderly friend, thaw meat for supper, water the lawn, etcetera.

This list varies from day to day and is treated informally.

Household chores, which bear an ugly sameness, day in, day out, can be treated more formally with a printed list with a space for a check mark when the duty has been fulfilled. I keep the list on computer disk and print out several months worth of daily work sheets at a time, crossing the task off when it's completed, discarding the sheet when its multi-day listings have been expended.

For optimum success for homemakers, work lists should be structured room by room and broken into a chronology so you have sheets for daily, weekly, monthly, and semi-annual chores. Formulating them by room allows you to centralize your actions, so you can move through your residence without a lot of wasted steps.

To prepare your worklist, wander through your house notepad in hand, and as you survey rooms jot what chores must be accomplished to halt the spread of Black Plague and keep the County Health Department from nailing a "Condemned" sign across your front door when you're embroiled in writing and don't even have time for lick-and-a-promise cleaning. Be realistic and fair with yourself when you decide with what frequency you must perform the various tasks. Chances are no one's paying you to do housework—and someone might be paying you to write.

For instance, cleaning the bathroom sink and vanity top are a daily necessity in our household. Wiping clean the rubberized bathroom scale surface is a weekly task. Cleaning dust from the bulbs inside the light fixtures can make do with semiannual attention. Whereas taking cleaning powder and an old toothbrush to the gears of the electric can opener are a biannual event for me and probably for you. (Unless you'd sooner be given a Bronzed Toilet Brush than have a shot at a Pulitzer.)

14.2   Let a Computer Lend a Hand

By having a standardized, neat work list on computer disks so I can print out fresh copies as needed, I spend less time "spinning my wheels," so to speak, and generate more time in worthwhile motion. The final outcome is a less cluttered environment that allows me to enjoy more serene, organized thought patterns as I write.

A psychological benefit that's most appreciated takes place on those days when I look around and can't see that I've accomplished a thing. At those times a glance at the work list with so many tasks completed will convince me (and my family) that I deserve an uninterrupted break at the keyboard.

Psyching yourself into writing when you don't feel like it, or believe you haven't the time, is one of a work schedule's finest traits. On days when I doubt I'll have a free moment, or happen to feel uncharacteristically lazy, or am suffering a mild case of The Big Block, I write "Work on manuscript" on my steno list. That reminder, prodding me, makes me feel compelled to work on something so that I can honestly cross it off the list. These bits of production, day by day, are what can mean the difference between success and failure in this competitive writing business.

14.3   Making Use of Child Labor

But perhaps a work list's crowning accomplishment is getting help from children—naglessly. Soon after I began my work scheduling with detailed lists clamped into a clipboard lying on the dining room table, miracles began to take place. Chores were done—and crossed off my list—without my performing them!

I discovered the allure of lists had attracted the kids like a new game. While I'm not a sweat-shop-type proponent of child labor— I'm certainly not one to refuse it, either.

Every day, every moment, life's opportunities await us, and in living through them we may garner a lot of great material to turn into salable 'scripts. For professional writers it's comforting and inspiring to realize that the desired hours are there waiting for us to *make* the time—and then *take* the time to write.

CHAPTER
15

Self-Motivation for Writers

Motivation, of course, is the reason or overwhelming impulse that causes a character to perform as he or she does under certain circumstances. Motivation, on the part of writers, is something quite different.

It's a process of removing lazy excuses not to write while placing emphasis on personal and professional reasons strong enough to insure that the author will set to paper the ideas forming in the mind.

15.1   Develop a 3-D Personality

Talent is important, but attitude is even more valuable. And a 3-D personality, comprised of Drive, Discipline and Determination, is a real boon if you wish to make it as a commercial writer.

Drive keeps a writer working hard and giving it his or her best effort.

Discipline keeps an author producing material day after day, year in, year out, and that is vitally important, because in the short story and nonfiction magazine market your future success depends on your present hard work.

Discipline also helps authors begin projects, and more important, finish them, as it can help alleviate a proclivity to procrastinate.

Determination enables a writer to work in the face of adversity. And it also provides the grit—stubbornness, if you will—to keep on marketing and to try and try again when a pet manuscript wings home rejected.

Determined people share a motto, one that writers might be well advised to script and hang in a place of prominence in the work area: *"QUITTERS NEVER WIN—AND WINNERS NEVER QUIT!"*

Over the years I've wondered just how many talented authors have thrown in the towel just one submission shy of approaching the market where they'd have succeeded. I suspect that their numbers are legion.

15.2 Writing away from Your Desk

To save time you can mentally write draft material in your mind while you do mundane household tasks that don't require full concentration, many of them touched upon in the last chapter.

Many writers will notice that they have a time of day when they're freshest and feel more motivated to do their best work. If you're one such writer, then pinpoint that time slot and be sure to schedule your day around it. And guard that valuable work slot with all the fervor of a Junk Yard Dog!

To succeed as a free-lance writer, it's imperative that you come up with a workable personal schedule. Then don't deviate from it except in an emergency. Keeping "office hours" (whatever yours might be) helps most writers establish a viable production routine.

15.3 Avoiding Time-Wasting and Money-Sapping Situations

It's especially valuable for writer/homemakers because those "office hours" help protect them from kaffe klatsch, home-sale parties and other time-killing, money-siphoning diversions, when all non-essential social obligations during your specific work period are refused.

Explanations to hostesses of home decorating, plastic-ware, lingerie, house-cleaning parties, that to a free-lance writer time-is-money, may win you a label as the neighborhood weirdo, but will preserve your time for writing. Get the word out that you're a serious professional writer (so local jobs may just come to you!). It might also preserve your time for working while conserving what finances you have to make them available for necessary things (postage, ribbons, paper, stamps, diskettes, even installment payments on a word processor) instead of eroding your cash flow for items you don't really want or need but feel obligated to buy in order not to look like a cheapskate, and are actually purchasing simply to salve someone else's ego.

15.4   The Quota System

In addition to selecting working hours you should also set a quota. The quota system is an invaluable psychological tool whereby the author promises to write a specific amount of literary properties in a set period of time.

For years my quota was two new manuscripts per week. In short order I had a very tidy backlog. Some weeks, I got really enthused, and I wrote more than the obligatory two pieces. Did I warrant time off for good behavior? No! The following Monday morning I began the new week facing a fresh quota.

The only way to make the quota system really work for you—and work it can—is if you'll be serious about it. Don't make excuses, especially not to yourself. With a quota you're on a personal honor system, and if you cheat yourself, you only harm your own best interests.

15.5   The Backlog Race

A spin-off of the quota system is the backlog race.

You don't have to go to Las Vegas to know that the more numbers you have on the roulette wheel, the better your chances of coming up a winner. By the same token, the more properties you have submitted that are under consideration with editors, the more likely your chances of acceptance.

At one time, I was almost fanatical about my backlog and for a year or more I maintained 50 manuscripts out circulating at all times. When a sale would come in, it would knock my backlog down a peg and therefore, in addition to the quota number, I also had to write a fresh piece to replace the "loss" as quickly as possible. Spurred on by an acceptance check, creativity really flowed.

Such a system worked beautifully, because it was not unusual for me to receive several acceptances per week, and once I received seven acceptances in one day.

These combined tricks kept me from ever resting on my laurels. The writing life is a continuous business. Things written now will pay off at some point in the future, so if you rest on your laurels and take time off for successful behavior, then inevitably you're going to suffer a dry spell when the period of inactivity catches up with you and you'll pay dearly, in the financial sense, at least, for that time off.

15.6 The 24-Hour Rule

I also lived by the 24-Hour Rule, and it was very helpful. If something came back rejected I made it a point to have it en route to another editor by the next day's outgoing delivery. I always made certain that I had on hand an ample supply of mailing envelopes, a goodly amount of postage, and the latest, most up-to-date marketing directory to make the task easier.

I also regularly visited magazine stores and idled away time looking at magazines that for one reason or another were not in the thick market directories. In addition, I asked relatives and friends to send me copies of unusual publications that were circulating in their areas, and I compiled my own market directory of regional publications not everyone knew about. Most of them used free-lance material, and some of their pay rates were exceptionally good. My sales record was solid because I was going where everyone else wasn't submitting, so my odds of success improved accordingly.

15.7 Success Begins with a Dream

Few people in this world hold down jobs for the sheer pleasure of laboring. Most show up at the workplace because they want money and the nice things that it can buy, or because they desperately need it to purchase bare necessities.

Writing is different. Granted, some authors do show up behind the keyboard because they're so thrilled with the act of creation. But for most of us, the prime motivation is money.

Think about the money that some famous authors make—then draw up a list of goals—things that you'd really like to have in life before it's "curtains" for you. Most of them will probably have a price tag attached. Maybe some of the best things are free. But items we want the most seem to require money.

Perhaps you simply want more cash at your disposal. Or you'd love to trade in your clunker on a new, snazzy car, and not face monthly payments. Perhaps you'll be facing sending kids to college in a few years. Or maybe you'd like to travel. All of those things do take bucks. Then again, in these times of high prices and job insecurity, perhaps your dream would be simply to make the wolf back a few more steps away from your door. Or it could be that your idea of really living is earning so much with your writing that you can buy what you want—without having to first ask the price.

Even pressing financial problems that could give average people an ulcer can provide an opportunity to authors sharp enough to use it as a motivating factor.

Stop to consider: most workers are on a set salary. They punch their time clock and collect a specific hourly wage. Writers are among the lucky people who can make their income fluctuate and who can earn almost outrageous sums of money for a few hours spent writing.

When it comes to writing you can earn a hefty sum—or you can earn a pittance. Basically your career is in your own control. Even if you're working a job already (and most sane writers, who want to remain that way do) when there is time in the month left over at the end of the money, a sideline business as a writer could do wonders in taking up the slack.

To keep yourself on target, goals are important, both long- and short-term ones. On New Year's Day, don't bother with personal, self-improvement resolutions that will only tarnish your self-image when you fail to run ten miles per week or refrain from eating sweets until the Fourth of July. Instead, make professional resolutions. Select a dollar amount you'd like to earn thanks to free-lance writing. Or, specify a number of manuscripts you'd like to create by year's end. Perhaps you even want to begin—and complete—a novel by year's end.

If you have a tangible goal written in your (all-important) notebook and carry it in your mind, as the months slip by you'll either be aware that you're on schedule, or know that you're slipping behind and will have to redouble your efforts to attain your goal.

15.8   A Little Help from Your Friends

Attendance at writer's clubs, subscriptions to trade journals, the purchase of instructional manuals and going to professional seminars can be very useful in helping you reach your goals. They'll bring inspiration, contact with people of like mind who share the joys and agonies of the writing life, and you'll very likely find someone you can relate to so that you can spur on each other with friendly competition.

Set a challenge. Have a race! If you're an unpublished writer and have a friend who is, too, promise that the one who sells a manuscript first gets treated to lunch by the other.

Treat yourself to a home study course, or buy a book or instruction or inspirational tape recording for writers, while vowing that you'll more than offset the cost of the wise investment in your career, because the inspiration and insight gained will allow you to recover the original cost many times over through compensation from future acceptance checks.

If you can open a savings account solely for your writing income, do so, and become infatuated with the figures. Nurture a desire to see the totals rise—and so will your production.

15.9 And Help from Within

There are many reasons to write, probably as many good ones as there are writers who desire to make it in the exciting publishing industry. Some reasons are:

- a need to create
- the urge to tell a story
- strong feelings about social problems
- a wish to share personal insights to help others
- a chance to amuse or entertain readers
- a challenging, enjoyable way to solve financial problems
- a desire to see your name in print
- a wish to become your own boss and have a sideline career
- seek "polite revenge" against those who scoffed when you sat down behind the keyboard
- the urge to be able to look friends and family in the eye, say, "*I am a writer*," and make the announcement without adding any self-doubting qualifiers or apologies.

So what are *your* reasons to write? Whatever the motivating factors that prompt you to produce, find them, use them, and then keep your eye on your goal and watch as your dreams become reality.

CHAPTER
16

The Markets and How to Approach Them

To get ahead as a free-lance writer it is imperative to treat it as the business it is—or certainly should be. To be accepted for publication it is necessary that you submit what you write, not secret it away in your desk drawer.

16.1   Don't Give Up

When I first began writing almost two decades ago, if a story or article came back rejected I didn't bother sending it out again because I was convinced it was no good, so I tossed the manuscripts into a drawer and wrote a new piece. Quite erroneously I believed that if one editor wasn't interested in purchasing the manuscript, another wouldn't be either.

One day, out of sheer desperation, I cleaned out the drawer, spent a small fortune in postage, and sent out over twenty submissions. Two weeks later, much to my surprise, I sold my first story—the second time it was submitted.

Now, many of my manuscripts sell on the initial submission, but others have sold only after as many as twenty-five trips to market.

16.2   Books to Tell You Where to Go

Writer's Market, published by Writer's Digest Books, *The Writer's Handbook*, released annually by The Writer, Inc., and *Inspirational Writer's Market*, a yearly reference book from Joy Publishers, as well as monthly market update sections in various writer's publications, serve as a wonderful resource to keep tabs on who's doing what in the publishing industry.

Not only do these collected works offer keen insight into what's timely in the publishing world but they also can give great inspiration because sometimes scanning market listings, and studying the helpful comments prepared by editors, can be almost like "taking an order," as it can give an author ideas of what to write and how to write it in order to find the straightest, smoothest, fastest route to success.

16.3 How to Make Your Approach

Care should be taken in preparing a manuscript for market. You have only one chance to make a good first impression. You wouldn't show up at a grand occasion wearing threadbare, dirty clothing. You'd dress your best. And so you shouldn't send a manuscript out tattered and disheveled. That gives it a shopworn appearance so an editor might assume it's been rejected by so many others that she isn't likely to be interested either, and might even return it unread.

16.4 A Bit About Editors

Editors do not have to read manuscripts. So long as they accumulate enough publishable pieces to print issues of their magazine, their bosses don't care if they don't read every word of each manuscript that arrives on their desks.

Therefore, it's a good idea not to give an editor a reason not to read your manuscript. As an instructor who must read submissions, there are times when I find myself shuffling manuscripts, postponing for as long as I can, reading the manuscript that's out-of-the ordinary.

A cover letter is a waste of time, or it can be a great sales tool, depending on what you have to say. As a rule I find it is not necessary to write a cover letter. Indeed, sometimes to do so can be a foolishly useless endeavor if you're writing one to tell the editor your story is enclosed. She can see that. Forget it, too, if you're merely stating that you hope she likes it. Obviously no one submits to an editor in hopes she'll despise the manuscript. And it's pointless to send a letter informing the editor that you hope she'll buy it. That goes without saying. That's what publishing is all about.

So unless you have something specific to state—like pointing out expertise that'll make the editor sit up and take notice, or impressive publishing credits that can give credence to your credentials as a writer—skip the cover letter and let your manuscript speak for itself.

16.5   Being in Good Form

Some common flaws are: single-spacing, space-and-a-halfing, instead of the standard double-spacing. Additional turnoffs are deleting words with X's or /'s instead of using an eraser, correction papers, or fluid. I feel vexed when authors send me manuscripts that are so faint I almost have to hold the paper up to the light to make out the impression. I have no choice but to read and critique the material, and a point I make to them is that editors are not that beholden, so they're their own worst enemies when they submit manuscripts that beg the recipient—out of a sense of eye-survival, if nothing else—to shove the messy manuscript into the SASE unread.

There are many good books and articles available that detail acceptable manuscript formats. Basically, a 'script should be typed, or printed, one side of the page only, on white standard-size paper, 20-lb. weight, double-spaced, with generous but not ridiculously large margins, using a dark ribbon, and if you have a dot matrix printer, set it on "near letter quality" mode, using a fresh ribbon. If the print is still faint, most dot matrix typefaces, if photocopied, will create an image that looks letter quality as copy machines can be adjusted to give a darker impression.

The author's name should appear on every page of the manuscript, and each page should be numbered, consecutively. Always keep a copy of the manuscript, whether it's a carbon, photocopy, or stored on computer disk.

In this era of computerization a number of authors use computer capabilities to save on postage, as they enclose a SASE with postage sufficient only for one ounce so that the editor can notify the author yes/no regarding the manuscript, and if the piece is unacceptable discard it, with the author considering it cheaper to print out a fresh copy than to pay to ship the rejected manuscript home.

16.6 The Facts About FAX

Faxing should be avoided unless an editor requests it, and many of them do if they want to see something or if they've requested revisions. But there's danger in faxing without permission to do so. The faxed piece may get tossed aside and never end up in the hands of the person meant to see it. And most businesses with faxes get quite a lot of "garbage" sent to their fax numbers, so your electronic submission could get discarded should someone fail to recognize it for what it is.

16.7 Preparing Your Properties to Be Posted

Manuscripts should be mailed flat in an envelope large enough to contain both it and the folded up SASE. Fold the return envelope neatly, in half, or by thirds. Do not fold the return envelope in quarters, or even worse, back in on itself for approximately one inch going around the perimeter of the return mailer. I can personally attest to how irritating it is to try to insert a manuscript into such an oddly creased envelope.

A very short manuscript, of five pages or less, can be mailed folded up in a No. 10-size business envelope. And in fact there can be some advantages to this. As the letter-size mail gets sorted and is opened first, it could obtain an editor's attention faster than if it's relegated to the manuscript stack.

Submit only one manuscript per envelope because to enclose two or more stories is like asking the editor to select which she likes the best, whereas mailing them individually may result in greater chances for both to be accepted.

Manuscripts may be mailed First Class Rate or by the more inexpensive Special Fourth Class Manuscript Rate. First Class postage is sold by the ounce, and Fourth Class by the pound, so for short stories it's usually no major savings to use Fourth Class postage. Addressing the issue as the wife of the Supervisor of Delivery and Collection at a Postal Sectional Center, I can assure you that the pennies saved may be no bargain at all when an author considers that First Class goes out immediately, whereas Special Fourth Class languishes in the post office until they have room to ship it out—a situation more likely to happen in metropolitan post offices than in those in small towns across the United States. Fourth Class sometimes travels as quickly as First Class, and other times it takes several weeks to go two thousand miles.

Plus, First Class is forwarded for a specific period of time after an individual changes their address, while Fourth Class is not. First Class is returned to the sender if it is unable to be delivered because the forwarding order has expired. Fourth Class is discarded unless the sender affixes notification, "Return Postage Guaranteed" beneath the sender's return address, at which point it will be delivered to the point of origin with the recipient agreeing to pay the fees upon delivery.

16.8 Do You Know Where Your Literary Children Are?

It is important to keep good records so you know what manuscript is submitted where and how long it's been there. If you log manuscripts in and out on a notecard in a small plastic or metal file box, you can tell at a glance where it's already been seen, and then move on to send it to editors who haven't yet had a chance to consider it.

You can quickly see if an editor has held the piece an inordinately long time. Sometimes manuscripts get lost in-office, usually if they're accidentally misfiled, or they may go astray in the mail system. There's always a chance, though, that the manuscript has been retained a long time because the editor really likes it, but just hasn't gotten around to accepting it yet and may've even lost track of time since the piece was received.

You can either send a polite letter inquiring about the manuscript and giving pertinent information (title, date submitted, your name and address) plus a SASE. Or you can pick up the phone and call the editor and ask for a "status check," then give your name, the title, the date submitted, and be prepared to wait for a minute or two while the editor checks the log or filing system.

16.9 Reach Out and Touch an Editor

If the editor has been holding the piece, a call can nudge her into taking action to make the final decision and either accept or reject a piece. If she's not ready to decide she'll tell you in a noncommittal tone that the piece is still in-office, but will make no additional comment. Bite your tongue, if you must, to keep from doing what editors hate, by asking, "Are you going to buy it?" when they aren't ready to commit themselves just yet and resent being put on the spot by a zealous author.

When you phone, keep business hours and varying time zones in mind, avoiding lunch hour and pre-office hours, or waiting until five minutes before quitting time to ask for a status check. Also, write notes so that you have the pertinent information directly in front of you so that you won't risk suffering the embarrassment of getting rattled, having your mind go blank and leaving you unable to supply even the most simple information. And have a pen handy to make notes on the same page if the editor imparts some interesting information.

Editors tend not to mind quick status calls because it spares them having to take time to write a note in response to a letter of inquiry—so it saves time—and it also gives the editor a chance to relate to you as another professional in the business, who happens to work from the other side of the desk.

Let the editor's attitude guide your call. If the editor seems inclined to talk—you'll know it, and you can profit from the pleasant interaction—you may gain valuable insights into how to succeed with her publication. In the same vein, if the editor does not wish to linger on the line, give polite thanks and end the call because she may've been conducting important business when she was interrupted.

16.10   Reading Between the Lines of Rejection Notices

Many publications use form rejection slips because the volume of material is so great that with reduced office staffs it is impossible to write a personal letter of rejection to each author. Therefore, if an editor writes even a word or two of encouragement on a printed rejection card, know that the editor was impressed about something in your manuscript, and that this is a subtle message to encourage you to submit to the magazine again.

If the editor writes, "Please try me again," that's a definite open door and it usually translates that the editor really liked your work—probably would've preferred to buy the manuscript—but perhaps wasn't able to due to scheduling problems, or a manuscript very similar in nature was already in inventory or assigned to another writer.

If the editor writes you a personal letter, pointing out weaknesses, and suggests that you might consider a rewrite, know that she is very interested in buying the piece if you can revise it to her needs. But she will not state this because she's not prepared to make that kind of commitment but is willing to take a chance on speculation.

So don't rewrite the piece and then send it to a different editor; return it to the one offering assistance as she assumes you'll do, in hopes that it'll result in a pleasant, mutually beneficial professional relationship.

The market for personal experience and true-life stories, in all categories, is wide open. Editors at many magazines are ready and eager to consider your manuscripts. So whether you write for money, to satisfy a need to create, for personal satisfaction, to offer solutions to a problem, or entertain and educate readers, the material is there—deep within you, or all around you—so write it and success can be yours.

APPENDIX A

Fictional Confession Story Markets and Guidelines

LEXINGTON LIBRARY, INC.
355 Lexington Avenue
New York, New York 10017

Dear Writer:

For JIVE and INTIMACY and BLACK SECRETS magazines, we strive for the stories to lean toward romantic lines. This does not mean that the stories should not have true-to-life experience plots. We simply want to project romance, love and togetherness, rather than to overwhelm our readers with violence or anything too depressing.

Make the stories believable. We do not want to deviate from reality. All endings cannot be happy ones, but we want to try, whenever possible, to cast an optimistic outlook as much as possible.

Hopefully, you can follow these guidelines and will soon be sending in your manuscripts. There is no limit as to how many you can submit at one time. It is good to submit material as frequently as you can, so that outlines for upcoming months can be made. However, if you send us an excessive amount of manuscripts to evaluate, you must be patient, for it will take us a longer period of time to get back to you. Here are the guidelines:

1. Stories must be written from a young, black, female perspective with romance in mind (this is not to discourage male writers, you may use a pen name).
2. Stories must be true-to-life confessions with interesting plots.
3. Stories need to exude an aura of romance.
4. Stories should have at least two descriptive love scenes. Each scene should be one page long.
5. Stories must be written in the first-person voice of the heroine.

6. Stories must be typed and double-spaced, with each page numbered and identified either with your name or the title of your work.
7. Each manuscript should follow professional manuscript format—including your name, address, and a daytime phone number.
8. Stories should be 5,100–6,000 words (17–19 pages).

Allow at least 3–6 months for confirmation of acceptance or rejection. If you need any assistance with writing a more romantic love scene, please call us at (212) 973-3200. We'll be glad to answer your questions. In our quest to give our books a more romantic look, we must enlist the help of our writers. We look forward to working with you.
(Payment rate Standard Confession Story—$75–100)

MACFADDEN WOMEN'S GROUP
215 Lexington Avenue
New York, New York 10016

The Macfadden Women's Group publishes MODERN ROMANCES, TRUE CONFESSIONS, TRUE EXPERIENCE, TRUE LOVE, TRUE ROMANCE, TRUE STORY.
Titles in the Macfadden Women's Group do not issue writers' guidelines. As an alternative they suggest that you pick up copies of their publications as the magazines themselves are the best indication of what they look for.
Manuscripts for all their publications must be double-spaced, good, dark typeface, and with acceptable stories ranging from an average 2,000–10,000 words. There is an average pay scale from 3 to 5 cents per word with a bonus of an extra $10 for accepted stories sent on an IBM-compatible computer disk. No byline is given and they acquire all rights worldwide. Handwritten stories are no longer accepted.
A large, self-addressed stamped envelope should be included for the manuscript's return. Writers are cautioned to retain a copy of the story in their own files in case something should happen to the original. Authors should allow at least an average six months for a reply, although a response might come before then or take longer.

Writers may enclose a self-addressed postcard with the submission if they wish to be notified of its safe arrival at the editorial office.

Stories must be written in the first-person viewpoint, and must be based on a true-life situation. Subject matter can be anything from light romance to current social concerns of interest to readers who are mostly working-class women. Some aspect of love or romance will usually figure in, but it need not be the primary focus as the characters face a conflict and solve a problem in their lives.

Some magazines also use seasonal and holiday theme poems and acquire filler material. The best way to learn of magazines' needs is to study current editions available at magazine racks nationwide, or by sending a check or money order for $2 to the specific title and request an issue of that magazine to study.

APPENDIX B

Writers' Organizations

There are a number of networking professional associations writers can join to band with authors of like interests for a furthering of professional concerns. Some organizations have stringent qualifications which must be met for membership and dictate whether the applicant can enjoy full membership or must be an associate member until additional professional qualifications can be fulfilled.

- American Society of Journalists and Authors, Inc.
  1501 Broadway, Suite 1907
  New York, New York 10036

- The Authors League of America
  234 West 44th Street
  New York, New York 10036

- National League of American Pen Women
  1300 17th Street N.W.
  Washington, D.C. 20036

- The National Writers Club
  1450 S. Havana, Suite 620
  Aurora, Colorado 80012

- National Writers Union
  13 Astor Place, 7th Floor
  New York, New York 10003

- Outdoor Writers Association
  2017 Cato Avenue, Suite 101
  State College, Pennsylvania 16801

- Writers Guild of America, East, Inc.
  555 West 57th Street
  New York, New York 10019

- Writers Guild of America, West, Inc.
  8455 Beverly Boulevard
  Los Angeles, California 90048

APPENDIX C

Market Listing References

Inspirational Writers' Market Guide, Joy Publishing, Box 827, San Juan Capistrano, California, 92675. Approximate cost, $20. A yearly market directory by Sally E. Stuart, covering the religious book and magazine publishers' needs, with helpful listings by denomination and region to direct authors to viable periodicals. Contains many markets not listed elsewhere.

Literary Market Place (LMP). Annual market directory published by R.R. Bowker, New York, New York. A national listing of book and magazine publishing sources, contains names of contact people, addresses, and toll-free telephone numbers. Does not contain detailed requirements stating publishers' needs. Approximate cost: $110.

Writer's Handbook, The Writer, Inc. Boston, Massachusetts, published yearly. Approximate cost, $30. Large reference work contains many articles devoted to the craft of writing, and covers 2,500 markets providing contact information in a brief format.

Writer's Market, published yearly by Writer's Digest Books, Cincinnati, Ohio. Available at bookstores for approximately $24, by direct mail, or *Writer's Digest Magazine* insert cards. *WM* lists most book and magazine publishers in the United States and Canada and contains a brief foreign section. A user-friendly, indepth reference work explaining publishers' needs in substantial detail.

APPENDIX D

Trade Journals for Writers

Byline Magazine, Box 130596, Edmond, Oklahoma 73013. Monthly general publication for freelance writers with a circulation of 2,000. Sample copy $3.

The Christian Communicator, Joy Publishing, 26131 Avenida Aeropuerto, San Juan Capistrano, California, 92675. For inspirational writers of interdenominational interests. Monthly newsletter, circulation 1,500, sample copy and guidelines for 9″ × 12″ SAE and two first-class stamps.

Christian Writers Newsletter, Box 8220, Knoxville, Tennessee 37996. Nondenominational bimonthly newsletter, circulation 400, a source of information and inspiration for Christian writers. Writers' guidelines and sample copy for No. 10 envelope SASE.

Housewife-Writer's Forum, Box 780, Lyman, Wyoming 82937. Support for women who juggle writing with family life, or for house-husbands who write. Bimonthly, circulation 1,300. Samply copy $4. Available by subscription only.

The Writer, 120 Boylston Street, Boston, Massachusetts, 02116. Monthly publication containing articles of a serious and literary nature. Sample copy $2.50 or available at magazine stores nationwide or by subscription.

Writer's Digest, F & W Publishers, 1507 Dana Avenue, Cincinnati, Ohio, 45207. Monthly publication, circulation 225,000, containing user-friendly, "nuts and bolts"-type articles covering all aspects of writing for pay. Sample copy $2.75. Available at

magazine stores nationwide or by subscription for approximately $21 annually.

Writers' Journal, Box 65798, St. Paul, Minnesota, 55165. Monthly
publication for free-lance writers, circulation 5,500, addresses
various aspects of writing for publication. Sample copy $2;
available by subscription.

APPENDIX E

Miscellaneous Resources for Writers

Educational Opportunities

Writer's Digest School, 1507 Dana Avenue, Cincinnati, Ohio 45207, or toll-free, 1-800-759-0963 for information regarding correspondence courses for writing nonfiction articles, short stories, novel writing, nonfiction book writing, and criticism service for articles, stories, books, and novels. Student works one-on-one with professional, selling author who specializes in the student's area of interest.

Christian Writers Guild, Norman B. Rohrer, Director, The Write House, Suite 1, Hume, California, 93628. Write for free starter kit and information.

Writer's Digest. May issue each year is devoted to available writers' conferences, listed by state.

How to Prepare Your Manuscript for a Publisher, David L. Carroll, Paragon House, New York, New York. This valuable handbook tells authors everything they need to know about professionally preparing a manuscript appropriate for submission to the marketplace.

Writing and Selling Magazine Articles, Eva Shaw, Paragon House, New York, New York. Brimming with insider information, this indispensable how-to manual shares techniques used by writers who make their living writing and selling magazine articles to diverse markets.

Supplies

Papyrus Place, 2210 Goldsmith Lane, Louisville, Kentucky 40218. Offers stationery supplies and hard-to-find items for the professional free-lancer. Send for free catalog.

Quill Corporation, Box 4700, Lincolnshire, Illinois 60197. Consumer-oriented wholesale supplier of authors' needs from A to Z. Send for free catalog.

Writer's Supply Club, Box 26524, Baltimore, Maryland, 21207, or call 1-800-732-1171 for free information.

About the Author

Susan C. Feldhake has been writing for almost twenty years and has sold over three hundred short stories and one hundred articles to a wide variety of national and international publications. She has also written both contemporary and historical novels, as well as several nonfiction books.

Mrs. Feldhake currently is on the staff of Writer's Digest School, and has previously worked as an agent for Illini Literary Agency, and as an editor and publisher of *Romantic Tidings for Inspirational Readers and Writers*, a trade journal. She is a member of The National League of American Pen Women, Romance Writers of America, and Novelists' Incorporated.

She lives on rural acreage with her husband, Steve, a postal supervisor, their children, and two very spoiled tomcats.